50 WAYS TO
HELP Y
COMM

Also by Steve Fiffer:

So You've Got a Great Idea

You Gotta Want It!

How to Watch Baseball

Against the Grain *(with Eugene "Mercury" Morris)*

A Season for Justice *(with Morris Dees)*

Hate on Trial *(with Morris Dees)*

Also by Sharon Sloan Fiffer:

Imagining America

50 WAYS TO HELP YOUR COMMUNITY:

A Handbook for Change

STEVE FIFFER
AND SHARON SLOAN FIFFER

MAIN STREET BOOKS

DOUBLEDAY
New York   London   Toronto   Sydney   Auckland

A MAIN STREET BOOK
PUBLISHED BY DOUBLEDAY
a division of Bantam Doubleday Dell Publishing Group, Inc.
1540 Broadway, New York, New York 10036

MAIN STREET BOOKS, DOUBLEDAY, and the portrayal of a building
with a tree are trademarks of Doubleday, a division of Bantam
Doubleday Dell Publishing Group, Inc.

Book Design by Gretchen Achilles

Library of Congress Cataloging-in-Publication Data
Fiffer, Steve.
    50 ways to help your community: a handbook for change /
Steve Fiffer and Sharon Sloan Fiffer.
        p. cm.
    "A Main Street book."
    1. Volunteer workers in social service—United States.
    2. Voluntarism—United States. 3. Social service—United States—
Citizen participation.   I. Fiffer, Sharon Sloan, 1951–
II. Title. III. Title: Fifty ways to help your community.
    HV91.F5   1994
361.3'7'0973—dc20   93-37989
                                                         CIP
ISBN 0-385-47234-X

Contents

Foreword

You don't have to take on the world. Shakespeare wrote, "How far that little candle throws his beams! So shines a good deed . . ." Gandhi said that revolutions occur through relationships. And Florence Griffith Joyner became the fastest woman on the planet by mastering an eleven-second race. Throughout history, the people who have accomplished the most have understood that real change occurs at the simplest thresholds of life: One moment. One deed. One relationship. The *where* of helping is simple.

But what about the *how*?

There are so many ways to help in your community. How should you begin? Should you select one specific need you want to address? Should you think about your own strengths—a head for business, a flair for the arts, a love of children—and find the best way to use them? Should you talk with neighbors, friends, family, teachers, or coworkers to get ideas about what's being done and how you can contribute? Should you read this book?

The answer to all of these questions is yes. This book offers you fifty terrific examples of ways to help. The people who did these things came up with them on their own. These are not fancy ideas; they're simple. And they can work.

As you read this book, decide which ideas you want to find out more about. Make some phone calls or write some letters. But most important, pay attention to which ideas you like. Not which ones you like in theory, but which ones make you want to get up out of your chair and get started. Notice what excites you. The way you help your community will be as specific and unique as your fingerprint, as personal as what matters most to you.

But why get involved in helping your community?

Because, as I know from my own experience, and as you will learn from yours, community service changes your life. It helps you to understand people with different backgrounds and different perspectives. When you understand those differences better, you will have a better understanding of yourself. You'll discover strengths you never knew you had. And you will form the kinds of bonds with other people that can only come from working together toward a common goal.

And as you change yourself through service, you will make an even more important change. Through service, you will help change your community, forever and for the better.

In September, President Clinton signed the National and Community Service Trust Act of 1993 into law, creating his new national service initiative, AmeriCorps. Before he signed the bill, the President spoke about this principle *why* of service.

"I ask you only now to remember . . . that it is at the grass roots, in the heart of every citizen that we will succeed or fail. Today we are taking a stand in this country for the proposition that if we challenge people to serve and we give them a chance to fulfill their abilities, more and more and more we will all understand that we must go forward together. This is the profoundest lesson of this whole endeavor."

As the President's words affirm, it is only by helping to transform our communities that we can make our country healthy, safe, literate, and free.

One moment. One deed. One relationship. One community. One country. Together we can take on the world.

ELI J. SEGAL
*CEO, Corporation for National
and Community Service*

Introduction

This is not a self-help book, but a book about selfless help.

There are books about how to make a million dollars. There are books about how to make love. This is a book about how to make a difference.

We all know the problems. We pass hungry and homeless people on the streets, lament the deteriorating public school system, bury our friends who have died from AIDS, worry about crime, the environment, battered women, abused children, the elderly, people with disabilities. The catalog seems endless—and so overwhelming that at times, whatever we might do to help appears almost futile. Can any of us really make a difference?

We can tell you from personal experience that the answer is yes! There are things, relatively simple things, we can all do. Last year we introduced and coordinated a free breakfast program at our daughter's elementary school. With the help of a remarkable corps of volunteers who helped purchase, prepare, and serve food (and read to the children while they ate), we fed forty hungry kids every morning for the entire school year. "Books and Breakfast" was one of the most rewarding experiences of our lives. More important, teachers reported that the children showed marked improvement in attentiveness, behavior, and academic performance.

50 Ways to Help Your Community is a starter kit for those willing to try to make a difference. For the past year we have combed the country looking for effective programs that you could become part of, replicate, or adapt in your own neighborhood, school, or workplace. In the following pages, you will meet fifty individuals or groups who have introduced these innovative yet simple ways to make the world a little better. For your convenience, a roster with brief descriptions of the people and programs is included.

The people profiled are not philanthropists or politicians, social engineers or social workers. They are ordinary men and women who believe that all of us must share our intellectual and creative resources to make our communities better places to live. Among them are a teenager in California who fosters racial understanding by pairing pen pals from different ethnic backgrounds; a grandmother in San Antonio who enlists senior citizens to teach and nurture latchkey kids after school; a group of professional women in Chicago who provide suitable clothing to women who are ready to find jobs; a group of African American men in North Carolina who serve as mentors to teens in need; members of a public school district in Washington who match needy students and business-people as lunchtime buddies; a group of employees in Tennessee who spend their lunch hours delivering meals to the elderly; and a modern-day Johnny Appleseed in Salt Lake City who organizes tree plantings and other environmental activities in urban areas.

The profiles are divided into three sections. In Part One, we focus on programs initiated by individuals and communities. Part Two describes school-related efforts—those created by students to help their peers and their communities and those designed by schools to meet the needs of their students. Part Three details community programs started by corporations and their employees and by professionals who use their particular skills to help those in need.

We feel confident that the stories of these courageous not-for-profit entrepreneurs will inspire you. But as Thomas Edison rightly noted, responding to the light bulb of inspiration is only a first step. Each profile also offers a blueprint and easy-to-follow instructions for participating in your community. Our Books and Breakfast diary in Chapter 16 is also designed to illuminate you about what it takes to get involved —the time, the legwork, the capital, the emotions, and the rewards. Finally, the appendix offers a resource guide to help you communicate directly with local and national volunteer centers and other programs that facilitate community involvement.

In the 1970s and 1980s we saw the dramatic rise of the "me-oriented" movement. But by the time President Bush left office in 1993, he had honored more than a thousand Americans as Points of Light for their volunteer work in their communities. In his inaugural address and on subsequent occasions, President Clinton has called us to a "season of service." By picking up this book you have demonstrated an interest in the new "selfless help" movement. May the pages that follow inspire you to make a difference.

Steve Fiffer and Sharon Sloan Fiffer,
October 1993

Roster

1. A TALE OF TWO CITIZENS

2. EDUCATION AND LITERACY

3. THE ENVIRONMENT

4. NEIGHBORHOOD SAFETY

PART 1:
Individual and
Community Initiatives

1.
A TALE OF TWO CITIZENS

A Person of Note

ELIZABETH CARTER AND TRI-STATE PROMOTERS

> **The program:** A tireless woman has transformed her once dilapidated block into a center for individuals in need. Different houses that she has rehabilitated offer food, clothing, shelter, and cultural enrichment to young and old.

Elizabeth Carter is on the telephone, describing her block in East Liverpool, Ohio. "It's not a wealthy neighborhood," she explains. "This is how it is. I'm talking to you from my home, that's 1180 Erie. Right across the street, 1177 Erie, is my husband Richard's barbecue business, and right next to that is the Adult Clothing House. A neighbor gave that house to me. Before he passed, he told me, 'You do so much good for the community, I want you to have it.' People give us so many clothes now, it's like a K mart. We run it on the honor system. The door is always open. Go in, sign your name, take only what you need, and please straighten up when you're done.

"Back on my side of the street, there's an empty lot—we keep it nice so children can play there. Then next to that is the Children's Clothing House. Same system as the Adult House, except when we get fancy clothes, we set a limit on what people can take. That building only cost two thousand dollars. It's worth more than that now. It was rundown, but we fixed it up, put a new roof on.

"Then there's another empty lot someone gave us. Then the house next to that, at 1192, I got from friends and we made a homeless residence; it's not a shelter, it's a home. All donated furniture. Very nice. There's an exchange student from Africa living there now.

"Then we skip a building, and at 1196 is our Creativity Center. We've got a group of beautiful women who help there. Every Friday they have arts and crafts for the children.

"Right across from that, at 1195, is Music House." Elizabeth pauses, like a mother counting heads to make sure she has accounted for all her children. Then, unable to conceal that she has a favorite, she bubbles: "That Music House is magic."

Why?

"Have you ever seen anybody angry when they're singing? No! It's good for the soul."

Elizabeth has been nourishing people's souls and bodies for most of her sixty-seven years. She currently provides food, shelter, music, and other educational, recreational, and cultural enrichment through the Tri-State Promoters, an all-volunteer, not-for-profit social service club she founded in 1965. It was about that time that she closed her small neighborhood delicatessen in East Liverpool, a town of 13,600 near the Ohio, Pennsylvania, and West Virginia borders, and opened a pantry providing free food to hungry neighbors.

The story goes that the delicatessen went under because Elizabeth was giving away too much of the food to kids in the neighborhood. Is it true? Elizabeth smiles. "I grew up in a family where we were all free-hearted. My mother says I got an overdose. What can you do with a hot dog on the grill? If you can't sell it, you can either throw it away or give it to someone who's hungry." She proudly notes that many of the youngsters she fed have gone on to become successful. "Ray Williams—his family was poor, poor, poor. Now he's an attorney in New Jersey."

With donations from stores and contributions from individuals and businesses, Elizabeth was able to keep the food pantry stocked and meet the needs of individuals and families in the community as they arose. She also organized Easter, Thanksgiving, and Christmas dinners where as many as one thousand hungry people were fed.

The food pantry, a block away on Pennsylvania Avenue, was followed by the Adult Clothing House and then Elizabeth's pet project, the Music House. She cannot remember the year she started the Music House, but she can remember the circumstances. "I was sitting on my porch looking at this old house across the street. There were kids hanging out there; it was just like a den of ill repute. I sat there and I thought, *This would be good for a music house.* So I talked to the gentleman who owned it, and he said he would need five thousand dollars cash. I said I couldn't do that, so he let me buy it on land contract. Took me a couple of years. It was a nice house, but the windows were broken out and it needed painting."

The local newspapers had been supportive of Elizabeth's food and clothing drives. A reporter she invited to see the future Music House told her the project would never work. But the newspaper ran a story, and the people of East Liverpool responded by donating three organs and four upright pianos. "The place doesn't look like the Marriott Hotel, but it's clean, and oh, it's a good feeling in there. A lot of love," says Elizabeth. She knows what she's talking about. She has been playing the organ in church since she was thirteen years old. "I've been playin' so long that people think I'm ninety," she says, laughing.

Music House is open every day. Volunteers, many of them retired teachers, work with five to ten children a day. The once-a-week piano and organ lessons are free, although donations are accepted. Lately, Elizabeth says, many senior citizens have been coming to learn to play the piano. "They're like the kids. Their parents wanted them to take piano when they were young, but they didn't want to. Now they're sorry." One older man whose wife had been taking lessons at the house for some time started dropping by after he lost his job. "At first he was very withdrawn, depressed. The music made a big difference. He opened up, started talking," says Elizabeth. "Music does that."

The success of the music program has inspired a number of other cultural efforts at Creativity House, including arts and crafts and dance. "A lady from Lisbon, Ohio, came and gave ballet classes," Elizabeth remembers. "Can you imagine ballet in a poor neighborhood?"

The ballet instructor was one of hundreds of volunteers who have assisted Elizabeth and her fellow coordinators Ann Johnson and Ruth Kincaid over the years. Additional support comes from the Chamber of Commerce, individual businesses, and local newspapers, which always feature the Promoters' initiatives. "We help every imaginable kind of person—black, white, red, yellow, green, it doesn't matter," says Elizabeth. "And our supporters and volunteers are of all colors, too. I know how some black people feel about racism today. I think the best way to deal with it is with love."

The Promoters have come a long way since Elizabeth started giving away hot dogs (she still gives snacks to kids in the neighborhood, but they have to pick up litter first). The home for the homeless cost $80,000, not $5,000 (a local couple, the Pusateris, and a bank provided essential support). And in May 1993, Elizabeth opened a cultural and entertainment center on Pennsylvania Avenue. There she features talent shows with children from the community.

The Promoters ask for a small admission fee at such events, but none of the money goes into Elizabeth's pocket. "You don't get paid for this kind of work," she says. Then she adds, "Well, in a sense you do, because inwardly I'm paid."

Is this inward compensation what moves her?

She thinks for a moment. "You just want to do it. It's a higher power that knows your heart. You can't be phony. I'm in this and can't help it."

For further information, contact
Elizabeth Carter, Tri-State Promoters,
1180 Erie Street, East Liverpool, Ohio 43920.

The Write Stuff

BRIAN HARRIS AND FRIENDSHIP SEES NO COLOR

The program: A youngster attempts to eliminate racial prejudice before it has a chance to begin by matching children from different ethnic backgrounds as pen pals.

I feel so lucky to be both black and white.
It gives me more time to sleep at night.
I don't lie awake with hate running in my head
Tossing and turning in my bed.

—from "Black and White," a poem by Brian Harris

When Brian Harris was seven years old, he attended a picnic sponsored by A Place For Us, a support group for multiracial families. He remembers that the picnic was fun because even though he had many friends at school and in his neighborhood, in this group, "I felt like I really belonged."

But for Brian, now an outgoing and resourceful young man of thirteen living in Stanton, California, the rich experience of growing up in a biracial family and socializing with others in similar situations was not an end in itself but a catalyst for his own inspired work. That work is promoting and coordinating Friendship Sees No Color, a club that he founded to match pen pals from different ethnic backgrounds. As Brian says, "Kids aren't prejudiced. They learn stereotypes from their parents and others, and if they don't know anyone who's a different color, they won't be able to find out what's true."

Brian had long spoken out against racism, sometimes surprising and unintentionally embarrassing classmates who didn't realize he was both African American and white. But he knew that speaking his mind wasn't enough, since he would never be able to touch everyone on his own. How could he reach more people?

The answer was less complicated than an adult might imagine. "A pen pal club," Brian says nonchalantly. "Anyone from anywhere can pick up a pen and write a letter. Besides, kids have to find out answers for themselves. This is a way of letting them do it one-on-one."

The concept was simple. But how could Brian reach all these potential epistolarians? Fortunately, his mature idealism does not detract one bit from his youthful savvy. He knew there was only one way to spread the word—only one method that instantaneously communicates to all people, of all ages, in all locations; only one tool that connects a kid in Montana with a kid in Mississippi: television.

Picking up his own pen, Brian wrote to every daytime talk show and news program, outlining his idea and requesting a forum. Although not every program responded, Brian soon learned that all it took was one national program to start a big ball rolling. When ABC's *Home Show* called and invited him to appear, both Brian and Friendship Sees No Color were on their way. He presented his idea before millions of viewers and invited young people of all ages to write to him and be matched with a pen pal from a different ethnic background.

Brian's parents, Smitty and Barbara, were supportive of his idea from the beginning. Fortunately, they had suggested that he use a post office box to receive correspondence. The box seemed full when three hundred letters arrived shortly after Brian launched the program on TV in February 1992. But that was a drop in the mail pouch compared to the ten thousand letters he received after a second *Home Show* appearance and the additional television and newspaper features that followed.

Brian acknowledges that one of the reasons for the huge response is that participation is easy. People interested in joining the club are simply asked to mail a self-addressed, stamped envelope and an index card with their name, age, sex, and race or ethnic background. Brian then matches pen pals, sending them information about each other. Initially he was confident he could answer the requests quickly. But because the majority of those writing are Caucasian, they often have to wait until an appropriate match arrives. Also, because Brian has school and homework and a normal life to maintain, he is practical about what he can and cannot do. "I know I might only be able to do about twenty matches out of a hundred in a night. But we do get it done when we can." His unpaid but committed staff includes his parents and his younger brother, Rodney. Although anxious to get started writing to their new pen pals, club members have been patient about delays.

Postal employees aren't always quite as patient, but Brian doesn't complain about them. He realizes he has made their job more complicated. He and his mother empty out P.O. Box 74 every morning before school, but Barbara still has to make a stop early in the afternoon to avoid the risk of an overflow of mail the next day. Brian remembers a time when they received a yellow slip informing them that there was too much mail for the box, and they went to the counter to retrieve three crates of letters. The postal worker suggested they pick up their mail more often. "She didn't know it was only one day's worth," says Brian.

Although there was no initial cost in starting Friendship Sees No Color, Brian says there have been expenses since the club's beginning. Some cards arrive without the self-addressed stamped envelope, and Brian does not want to punish the offenders. Contributions from friends and unsolicited donations from those who have seen or read about the effort cover the cost of extra postage and supplies as well as the post office box.

When the family needed help to cover additional expenses, they brainstormed and came up with another idea to raise money. Club members can now buy T-shirts that spread the word with the Friendship Sees No Color logo, designed by the prominent Chicago cartoonist Adrienne Sioux Koopersmith. Merchandising, however, will never be the purpose of the club, Brian emphasizes.

The mission remains simple and to the point. Brian wants to eliminate prejudice. And, most important, he wants to eliminate it before it begins. In waging this battle, he is anxious for all the help he can get. He is interested in finding statewide directors who can help publicize Friendship Sees No Color by becoming area spokespersons, contacting the media, and searching out potential pen pals. Young people interested in helping Brian coordinate the effort should take their own pen to paper and write to him. Young people interested in attacking a different social issue through a pen pal club or by some other means should be inspired by his success. The rewards of helping people are tremendous, Brian says. "I know I'll never make any money from this. I know it's not going to be a profitable career. But I know that people are hearing my message."

Those wishing to find a pen pal, start a chapter, or learn more should contact
Brian Harris, Friendship Sees No Color,
P.O. Box 74, Stanton, CA 90680.

2.
EDUCATION AND LITERACY

Starting Young
SHIRLEY MOSINGER AND BEGINNING BABIES WITH BOOKS

The program: Volunteers visit every new mother, many of them young and poor, in a public hospital to discuss how reading develops a child's interest in learning. They give children's books to the mothers free of charge, offer advice on how to read to children, and, when appropriate, provide information on adult literacy programs.

Shirley Mosinger recalls the exact moment that she conceived the Beginning Babies with Books program. "It was 1988," says the sixty-two-year-old mother of four from St. Louis. "My newest grandson was exactly six weeks old. He was lying on the changing table looking at me, and I was looking at him. I said, 'Hi, Tyler,' and smiled at him, and he just got so animated. His little legs started going, and he wiggled and cooed. I realized that if I hadn't said anything, he'd just be lying there, not engaged at all. And I thought, somebody has to tell all new mothers how important it is to talk to their children from birth, *and that somebody has to be me.*"

The notion that parents should talk to their babies seems at first obvious. But as a longtime volunteer in the St. Louis public schools, Shirley was well aware of studies indicating that many parents either don't realize that communicating with their children from day one is essential or don't have the energy to do so. Parenting, she notes, is not a natural talent, or an easy skill to learn. "It's surprising how many people still treat infants as objects, as something merely to be fed and diapered, and don't talk to them," she says.

In addition to volunteering in the schools, Shirley had long tutored for local literacy organizations. Working with adults who could neither read nor write, she had become particularly frustrated by the intergenerational cycle of illiteracy. "In St. Louis, as in most cities, 35 percent of those sixteen years or older don't have high school diplomas," she explains. "Many of them are illiterate. And if parents or a single parent can't read, it's very probable that their children won't be able to read." Furthermore, studies show that children who are read to at an early age gain a greater understanding of language and its uses than those who have little early contact with books.

As Shirley held her young grandson, she realized that the need for new parents to talk with their babies and the need to break the intergenerational cycle of illiteracy might be joined in a single initiative. And thus, Beginning Babies with Books was conceived.

Unfortunately, gestation took considerably longer than nine months.

Shirley had little difficulty in shaping her idea. Research quickly revealed that mothers who were young, economically disadvantaged, and single parents were most in need of a program. Where could such mothers be found? On the maternity ward of St. Louis Regional Medical Center, the area's largest public hospital—a captive audience if ever there was one.

Shirley drew up a one-page proposal for "a program to establish literacy as a value for every new mother at the Medical Center, to teach new mothers how to read to their child, to provide the books a new mother needs to start a reading program at home, and, when appropriate, to encourage the new mother to attend literacy classes." Volunteers trained by literacy and early childhood experts would talk with the mothers and give them written information about the benefits of reading and three free children's books. There were 3,500 births at the center each year. Shirley calculated that it would cost $10,000 annually to buy books and printed material.

She also realized that the program needed an energetic, committed, unpaid volunteer coordinator—a role she was eager to assume. "It sounds trite, but I think it's really important that we all try to make the world a better place. I kept thinking of the old adage that if you give a man a fish, he eats for one day, but if you teach him how to fish, he eats for the rest of his life. Literacy is like fishing. At its most basic level, it is educating someone in how to earn a living."

The medical center administrators who read the proposal were interested in starting the program, but as Shirley had expected, the hospital had no money to fund it. Figuring that it would be easier to find funding through an existing organization than to create a new one, she approached the literacy group where she had worked. To her surprise, the organization turned down the proposal. "They told me their focus was on adults, and my idea had to do with children," she says. She approached another service organization where she had worked, but it was strapped for cash.

Shirley and her husband considered putting up their own money and soliciting friends to get the program started, "but we realized that that would only work for a year, and there was no point in starting something if it wasn't going to be ongoing." So despite Shirley's enthusiasm, Beginning Babies with Books could not begin. "I can't tell you how frustrating it was," she says. "Here was this idea—so simple, so basic, so easy. I kept asking myself, *Why can't we do this?*"

As Shirley contemplated other funding possibilities, she learned of the imminent birth of a new organization in Missouri—LIFT (Literacy Investment for Tomorrow), a statewide not-for-profit agency that would advocate and fund literacy efforts with money solicited from the private sector. LIFT's executive director-to-be was Diana Schmidt, an old friend from the St. Louis literacy movement. Shirley approached her before the new organization was officially in operation.

Diana saw the benefit of reaching new mothers and said she was confident that she could find corporate support for Beginning Babies with Books. Soon after LIFT opened its doors in 1990, Diana delivered. "We need to take steps like this to insure that children develop a love of reading and learning at an early age," she says, adding, "There's a double benefit. By encouraging the mother to read, we also stress the importance of the parent's being educated."

How does the program work? Shirley placed advertisements in local newspapers, called on friends, and worked through the medical center to develop a corps of volunteers, which now numbers ten at any given time. Before visiting new mothers, these volunteers go to the center for a three-hour training session that includes talks from a representative of the city schools' early childhood education program; a representative from Parents and Teachers in the Home, an organization that visits parents in the home; Diana Schmidt; hospital administrators, who describe the patients and the center rules; and Shirley. The volunteers are also given literature about the importance of reading to children.

Once trained and provided with books and other material for the mothers, the volunteers are ready to begin. The average visit takes about two hours. They talk to the mother and whoever else might be in the room—the baby's father or siblings or the mother's friends or relatives.

Because of budget limitations, new mothers receive two books instead of three. These books, purchased in bulk from a local wholesaler, include a cardboard number or letter book that the baby can hold (or chew!) and a simple storybook appropriate for the baby and its young siblings. "Most of the mothers have other children at home, and we figure we can reach them too," says Shirley. "One mother looked at me and asked, 'Where were you eight years ago, when my first one was born?' "

As the seven thousand babies whose mothers have received books during the program's first two years will not enter school for another three years, it is difficult to quantify the success of the program so far. Follow-up calls to mothers do indicate that they are using the books. In addition, several parents have asked for information about adult literacy programs. Recently, volunteers have begun to provide mothers with library card applications; follow-up reveals that many new cards have been issued.

While Judy Sams, the center's director of volunteer services, provides valuable support, Shirley remains the soul of the operation. After putting in "countless hours" bringing the program to fruition, she still spends about four or five hours a week visiting mothers and recruiting and coordinating volunteers. "This is my dream fulfilled," she says. And then she tells the story of a visit to a room where a father sat holding his new daughter. "He thanked me for the books and then he looked down at his little girl and said, 'This child is going to college.' "

LIFT-Missouri has produced a manual for initiating a similar effort at any hospital, and Judy Sams has talked to several hospitals around the country about the program. For further information, contact Judy Sams, Director of Volunteer Services,
St. Louis Regional Medical Center,
5535 Delmar Blvd., St. Louis, MO 63112.
Phone: 313-879-6233.

Supply-Side Education

NICK MONREAL AND TEACH THE CHILDREN

> **The program:** Individual volunteers and service organizations raise money to purchase school supplies for young students whose families cannot afford them. Volunteers also solicit school supply manufacturers, wholesalers, and retailers for product donations. The supplies are then turned over to the schools, which distribute them without stigma to needy children.

The scene in the San Antonio elementary school classroom puzzled Nick Monreal. A well-dressed student had walked from his desk to a wastebasket and tossed in a crumpled piece of notebook paper. Moments later a classmate, not dressed nearly so well, quietly rose and approached the receptacle. He looked around to see if anyone was watching. Convinced that no one was observing him, he removed the crumpled paper and took it back to his desk. There he studiously smoothed it out.

What is this? wondered Nick, who at that time, in 1976, was a program monitor and evaluator for the local Department of Human Services. Had the first boy left a secret message for the second?

As Nick sauntered casually toward the scavenger, he noticed that the boy was erasing the writing on the paper. This task finished, he began working on an assignment.

Nick approached the boy and gently asked what was going on. The student, obviously uncomfortable, confessed that he had no paper of his own. Why? Because his family could not afford it, or other school supplies.

Nick went to the teacher. Didn't the school provide supplies for those unable to purchase them? No, she informed him. If supplies were given to needy kids at all, in this or any other school she knew of, they were paid for out of the teacher's own pocket.

Nick did a little mathematics in his head. He knew that there were thousands of children in the San Antonio school system who qualified for free or reduced-rate lunches because of the financial plight of their families. He reasoned that most of these families would also have trouble paying for paper, pens, pencils, rulers, and notebooks. No doubt there were millions nationwide facing the same predicament—resigned to hoping for a beneficent teacher or a wasteful classmate. How, he wondered, could these students—stigmatized, embarrassed, and without the necessary tools—hope to perform adequately?

"It was this one visit to the school that gave me the idea for Teach the Children," Nick says. "I realized that in our country we have laws that provide for the free education of all children, but nothing to provide for the necessary materials to support that instruction." Nearly two decades later, this is still the case. A 1990 study by the Carnegie Foundation found that almost 70 percent of U.S. schoolteachers spend more than $100 of their own money each school year on supplies, 45 percent spend more than $200, and a full 15 percent spend more than $500 per year. Still, far too many children are without the supplies required to do their classwork.

Having worked in the social service field most of his adult life, Nick knew he could not solve every child's problem immediately. He narrowed his focus to his own community and within that community targeted "those children whose parents had exhausted all avenues of getting supplies." Conversations with local administrators revealed that not only were many children performing poorly because of inadequate supplies, some were even dropping out of school.

Most people who become involved in their community claim that it is better to establish a new program under the auspices of an existing agency, if the agency is willing and capable. Initially, Nick had no intention of starting his own not-for-profit organization. But when he proposed a school supply drive to his superiors in the governmental agency, they turned him down, for reasons never fully explained.

Fortunately, at the same time Nick was serving as interim director of a federally funded antipoverty community action program called CAP West. This organization could sponsor the initiative he had in mind—if he could build a case that surpassed mere personal observation and anecdotal tales. He began by contacting the local teachers' union and teacher organizations. Long condemned to purchasing supplies with their own funds, the teachers were understandably enthusiastic. So too was the school district.

In some school systems, students who receive free lunches are publicly identified; their lunches are marked with blue tags, distinguishing them from the lunches of those who can afford to pay. Nick did not want to embarrass children in need of supplies further, and he did not want to compromise the credibility of the program by giving the impression that it was to be a mass giveaway. He therefore determined that the supplies should be distributed quietly and privately within the school system.

With the support of school administrators, teachers and social workers identified deserving students. Applications for assistance were then sent to these students' homes. "Unfortunately, many of the parents were too proud to sign the forms," says Nick. "So I sat down with parents and teachers and said, 'The kids shouldn't be penalized by this.' " A process giving the school the authority to distribute supplies without parental permission was then established.

But where would the supplies come from? At the same time that Nick was working with the schools, he was considering different means of securing the supplies. His first attempts to raise money from individuals were not successful. But several retailers whom Nick approached were willing to donate surplus supplies or damaged goods. The program started slowly. During the early years, an average of 150 children were given school supplies annually.

By the mid 1980s, however, that number had jumped to almost ten thousand. How? In 1981, KENS, the local CBS television affiliate, offered to do a telethon to raise money for the effort. Such television station/community partnerships were not unusual at the time. To keep their licenses, stations had to provide a certain amount of community programming. For several years, the telethons raised between $40,000 and $60,000 for the program. By this time the original sponsor, CAP

West, had fallen victim to the budget cutting of Reaganomics, and Nick had created a separate not-for-profit corporation, Teach the Children.

The organization was off and running. In April and May the schools would identify needy students. Before the beginning of the next school year, Nick would use the funds raised by the telethon to purchase supplies at wholesale prices.

Although Teach the Children was able to flourish without government funding, it eventually suffered from the federal deregulation of the broadcast industry. When community affairs programming requirements for local television stations were relaxed, KENS evaporated as a funding source because it was now able to sell the precious air time previously devoted to the telethon.

Once again Nick had to hustle for supplies or the money to buy those supplies. He organized numerous fund-raising activities, among them selling fajitas at local fairs. He successfully solicited San Antonio–based companies. He persuaded several stores to set up bins in which customers could donate supplies. And he worked out a creative arrangement with Krogers, the popular supermarket chain. Rather than contribute money or supplies, Krogers offered to promote Teach the Children in its advertising. Nick's legwork was rewarded. Despite the loss of the telethon, he was able to provide supplies to more than three thousand children . . until Winns Stores, Inc., made him an offer he couldn't refuse.

Winns Stores, a large five-and-dime retailer in Texas, sold Nick goods from its warehouse at attractive wholesale prices and also asked its suppliers to donate material. In 1987, the company's community relations staff, with whom Nick maintained regular contact, presented an even more attractive offer: Winns would contribute the proceeds from a one-day warehouse sale to Teach the Children. The proceeds would go directly into a special account from which the organization could buy supplies at a discount from Winns. The company did ask Nick to find volunteers to sell hundreds of items, ranging from ice chests to plants to bicycles. He did, and soon an annual event raising between $35,000 and $45,000 was in place.

Not surprisingly, between coordinating the warehouse sale, recruiting schools, and purchasing and delivering supplies, Nick was devoting almost as much time to Teach the Children as he was to the Main Plaza, a restaurant he had opened in the 1980s after leaving the directorship of CAP West. His wife, Diana, and teenage children, Nicholas, Denise, and Daniel, were also volunteering their time for Teach the Children. In 1990 the economic downturn and local street repairs that made access to the restaurant very difficult forced Nick to consider closing the Main Plaza. But what would he do to make a living?

Diana Monreal told her husband that she knew how much he believed in Teach the Children and how he dreamed of taking the concept beyond the San Antonio area. She suggested he raise additional money to support himself as the organization's director while he tried to expand the program statewide or nationwide.

Nick had been thinking the same thing. "I told her that with the struggle for the restaurant, I was being tested to see how sincere I was about Teach the Children," he recalls. "I told her, 'I can't let it go down just because the restaurant is going under.' "

Still, Nick had his doubts about continuing. To expand the concept throughout the state and at the same time earn a minimal living would require state funding. And that would require writing a grant proposal. "I told Diana I hadn't written a proposal for government funding in ten years," he says.

Diana responded, "That's what you have friends for." She was right. With the help of friends who knew about writing funding proposals and the use of statistics indicating the staggering number of poor children in the Texas public schools, Nick was able to convince the state to award Teach the Children money to promote and supervise expansion. A modest amount was allotted for Nick's salary to run the program.

Nick's enthusiasm and knowledge and the program's simplicity made selling other school districts on the idea relatively easy. There were barriers, however. Some administrators and school boards had to be persuaded there was indeed a need. Nick was prompt to point out that in its first decade alone, the organization had helped 144,000 children who had been certified by their schools. At first some schools perceived Teach the Children's efforts as interference rather than assistance. Testimonials by satisfied administrators usually convinced these doubters.

Statewide expansion progressed. Governor Ann Richards declared 1991–92 "Teach the Children Year." And Nick dreamed of chapters across the country. That dream became a reality, thanks in large part to a service organization and a soft-drink manufacturer.

The service organization is Circle K, whose chapters on college campuses across the country help students participate in community programs. Prior to a 1991 convention that happened to be in San Antonio, Circle K's Lisa Fargo contacted the San Antonio United Way to ask about local not-for-profits that might be of interest to members. The United Way mentioned Teach the Children.

Nick was asked to address the convention. He prefaced his remarks by showing an eight-minute documentary film about Teach the Children that had been produced by the local PBS station. The audience gave Nick a standing ovation. Nick was equally impressed with the organization. Those attending a dinner dance at the convention were asked to bring school supplies as their "admission ticket." They responded with enough material for two hundred children.

Representatives of Circle K chapters across the country told Nick they would get more supplies and send them to Texas. He suggested an alternate plan: these service-minded college students should help establish Teach the Children programs in their own communities. With Nick serving as an unpaid consultant and motivator, Circle K chapters, along with Key Club, the organization's high school affiliate, have started programs in more than twenty-five states.

Nick's effort to go beyond the college communities where Circle K is involved has been helped immeasurably by Coca-Cola, which knows the real thing when it sees it. Having received some support from Coca-Cola U S A.'s marketing division over the years, Nick sought funding from the corporation to take Teach the Children national. He received a generous five-year grant that will cover his administrative and travel expenses.

The grant also provides Nick a modest salary. He realizes he could earn more in the private or even governmental sector, but he has no complaints. He is happy to devote the rest of his life to providing children with the means for doing their best in school and breaking out of the cycle of poverty. He tells the story of a fourteen-year-old boy who was the sole breadwinner in his family. Any money that might have been allotted for school supplies was instead used to put food on the table at home. The boy was a good student, but the lack of supplies, along with the burden of supporting the family, was causing his school-work to suffer. Teach the Children was able to remove at least one of those concerns. Then there was the family in which the students were so embarrassed by their inability to afford supplies that they would not go to school. Again, Teach the Children was there.

To those who don't think twice about purchasing supplies for their children, these problems might be difficult to fathom. To those who complain about the high cost of such supplies, the problems of allocating enough money for school supplies might be more understandable. To the principal of one school helped by Teach the Children—a school where 93 percent of the students receive free lunches—the lack of paper, pencils, and rulers is the rule, not the exception.

Like many efforts to help in the community, Teach the Children is successful because of its simplicity: children need school supplies to perform better; let's get them supplies. Such an effort can easily be started or replicated in any school district. Nick is happy to provide assistance. "It may sound corny," he says, "but we all have a reason for being here. This is mine."

Nick is expanding Teach the Children to school systems around the country. For further information, contact
Nick Monreal, Teach the Children,
7249 Bandera Road Suite D, San Antonio, TX 78238.
Phone: 210-680-0217.

After-School Special

HENRY AND MARY ANN GASKINS AND FREEDOM YOUTH ACADEMY

The program: A husband and wife have virtually turned their home into a school. Each day after work and for several hours on Saturday, they tutor and enrich inner-city students of all ages. Their own children and other "peer tutors" assist. The not-for-profit academy places special emphasis on preparing high school students for the Scholastic Aptitude Test, a standardized college entrance examination.

Henry and Mary Ann Gaskins never planned on turning their house into one of the foremost after-school learning centers in the country. Still amazed at the events of the past decade, Henry says with a shrug, "It just grew." Mary Ann adds that they have no regrets that the rec room, dining room, and upstairs den in their beige brick split-level home in Washington, D.C., have become classrooms where as many as seventy-five children study each day.

The Gaskinses' Freedom Youth Academy began growing in the moonlight of the second job Henry took to help feed and educate their own five children. A minor-league catcher before major-league baseball was fully integrated, Henry left the game in the mid-1950s, earned a Ph.D. in adult education, and started a day job at the Library of Congress. To earn enough money to put his own kids through college, he took an after-hours job helping affluent suburban high school students get into the colleges of their choice. For $35 an hour he tutored these would-be Ivy Leaguers to improve their class rank and test scores.

Henry's students achieved excellent results. But while he found the tutoring both professionally and financially rewarding, he was not completely satisfied. Back home in the southeast quadrant of the city, his own children were doing well in school. Some of their friends were having trouble, however, particularly when it came to getting into their first-choice colleges. Although these students, most of whom were black, earned good grades in high school, they did not perform well on the SATs and lacked adequate communication skills. Henry had learned this firsthand when helping several high school seniors from the neighborhood fill out their college applications.

Henry chose not to focus on what many educators have identified as cultural discrimination in aptitude tests that has an adverse effect on minorities. Mathematics is color-blind, he reasoned, and he could not change whatever bias might exist in the verbal skills sections of the tests. But there was something he and Mary Ann, a NASA consultant, could do. He remembers, "I'd been coming home every night with success stories about these suburban kids getting into Yale and Harvard, and my wife said there should be more of that in our local schools. We began talking about bringing the tutoring concept I was using in the suburbs into the inner city."

Those talks raised many questions. What age students would the Gaskinses attempt to assist? Where would they find these students? What would they teach them? Where would they teach them? When would they teach them? Would they charge any money for the program? Could Henry afford to give up his lucrative evening tutoring job to work with these students?

Surprisingly, the answers came naturally and quickly. Henry would take a leave of absence from his night job to work with Mary Ann on a program that would offer high school students a little recreation and a lot of tutoring and SAT preparation. The Gaskinses would charge $5 per session, but those unable to pay would not be turned away. The Gaskinses would operate the not-for-profit program out of their home and enlist their children to assist in the tutoring. The couple would take advantage of the federal government's flexible hours system and work at their day jobs from 7:30 A.M. to 3:30 P.M., then rush home to meet the students after school. They would also tutor on weekends. They would recruit students through their own children, in the neighborhood, and through the high schools.

About fifteen high school students showed up for the first day of the Freedom Youth Academy. Henry concentrated on the boys; Mary Ann worked with the girls. Although the students were eager to work, they were, says Henry, surprisingly deficient in the basic skills. "So we decided that we had better start with seventh graders." Unfortunately, the Gaskinses soon saw that those in junior high were also far behind where they should be. "We felt we had to go back even further to try to help these kids before it was too late," says Henry. The academy began offering different programs for students from kindergarten through twelfth grade. Enrollment rose to more than seventy-five students. Different age groups came at different times, but still they filled every space in the house but the bedrooms.

Almost fifteen years later, both the house and the Gaskinses, who are now in their fifties, are still standing, and students are still coming to the academy. Adult volunteers and students willing to tutor their peers or younger children assist the couple. Among these student tutors is Kendra Gaskins, who will soon follow her four older siblings to college.

Each of the Gaskins children has enjoyed academic success, and so too have hundreds of inner-city students who have learned everything from how to read to how to prepare for the SATs at the academy. Over 80 percent of the students have achieved some kind of academic recognition at their schools, such as honor roll or dean's list, and every student who has completed Henry's eight-week SAT course has gone on to college Several have joined the suburban kids whom Henry once tutored at such institutions as Brown, Smith, and the University of Pennsylvania. Academy students taking the course raise their SAT scores anywhere from 50 to 360 points. Charles Dabney, who attended the academy from sixth through twelfth grade, is a typical success story. At Banneker High School he maintained a perfect attendance record and won his class leadership and service awards, in part for his work as a peer tutor at the academy After taking Henry's course, he increased his SAT score 340 points, to 1230 (out of a possible 1600), and was accepted at Drexel University in Pennsylvania.

The Gaskinses have received numerous awards for their tireless work, and in recent years their not-for-profit organization has attracted corporate and foundation support that has allowed them to purchase computers and other needed equipment and supplies. While they don't expect others to commit as much time and energy (and house space!) to enriching the lives of inner-city kids, they do hope their story will inspire those on the sidelines to become more involved. "You don't have to be an expert," says Henry. "You just have to believe that it is essential to instill kids with the importance of education. You don't have to put in the hours we do. Take one child to the library. Help one child learn how to read. These will make a difference."

**For further information, contact
Henry and Mary Ann Gaskins, Freedom Youth Academy,
1405 34th Street SE, Washington, DC 20020.**

3.
THE ENVIRONMENT

From the Ashes
PEPPER PROVENZANO AND TREEUTAH

> **The program:** Volunteers plant trees to improve the environment and the quality of life in and around the population centers of Utah. The organization they have formed serves as a clearinghouse to facilitate planting projects, lends technical support and helps oversee community plantings, organizes and mobilizes citizen participation, and educates the public on environmental issues. TreeUtah volunteers have planted almost fifty thousand trees since 1989 and hope to have planted two million by the year 2000.

Visit Utah on Earth Day and you will find hundreds of TreeUtah volunteers planting thousands of seedlings in order to reforest the Wasatch Mountains. Visit in early October and you will find hundreds of households joining with local nurseries to participate in Plant Your Family Tree Week. Travel to the Beehive State for the Christmas holidays and you will find hundreds of citizens purchasing live Christmas trees and donating them for planting in city parks and cemeteries. And visit almost any weekend and you'll probably find at least one city neighborhood where residents are planting trees to beautify their surroundings. Such efforts, representative of the urban forestry movement burgeoning across the nation, are the direct result of an unassuming yet committed Salt Lake City resident named Rick "Pepper" Provenzano—and they are easy to replicate in any community.

It took years for the hundreds of ash trees in Salt Lake City to reach their full majesty. It took one day for a municipal forestry crew to cut down the first six of these towering ashes, which were thought to be diseased or to be likely to become diseased. And much to his own amazement, it took less than a minute for Pepper Provenzano to "go ballistic" and decide he had to do something to save the trees on his front parkway and throughout the city. In this explosive moment, the seeds of TreeUtah were planted.

Before Pepper met the forestry crew in his front yard on a warm spring day in 1987, his involvement in community affairs had been negligible. A wire editor for Salt Lake City's major newspaper, the *Tribune,* he had previously helped with a newsletter for people with hearing impairments and had participated in developing a public service announcement for the local Special Olympics.

Pepper, now forty-three, admits that while "the idealism I had from growing up in the sixties never left me," he felt a bit guilty and empty because he had not found a cause to arouse his dormant passions. He appreciated nature, having fallen in love with the desert of Arizona while in college and the mountains of Utah after moving to Salt Lake, but he had never been an ardent environmentalist. And like many who do become active in their communities, his first steps were motivated by personal, not global, concerns. Quite simply, he loved the two seventy-five-foot ash trees in front of his house. They provided shade as well as relief from the dust, sound, and visual pollution between his house and the busy street. And their beauty not only pleased him but enhanced the value of his property.

When the tree-cutters asked Pepper to move his car so they could bring in their equipment, he refused and demanded to speak to their supervisor. They referred him to the city forester. "I called him right away," Pepper remembers. "I said, 'I don't know what my rights are, but I want a second opinion.' " The forester told him he would grant the trees a reprieve until the city Forestry Board's next meeting, in two weeks. At that time Pepper would be welcome to present his case for clemency.

Pepper sought help from a logical source. "I went to the arboretum " There he was advised that many of the trees in his neighborhood probably should come down; they were infested because of old age and needed topping to clear high-voltage power lines. But he was also told that several trees should not have been targeted. "They had another twenty years left," Pepper says.

When Pepper presented these findings to the Forestry Board, he again confessed that he was uncertain of his legal standing. "I said, 'I don't know the letter of the law, but I know its spirit,' " he recalls. The board agreed to continue the trees' stay of execution and assigned a staff member to go through the neighborhood with Pepper and evaluate each ash.

What began as an adversarial relationship quickly turned into a cooperative effort, particularly after Pepper learned that the forester and his five-man crew were responsible for the fate of some fifty thousand trees in the city. "Five men! That's ridiculous," says Pepper. Although the forester received some federal money for tree removal and limited replanting, he had not had the manpower to evaluate each ash. Understandably, although sadly, he had therefore condemned all the trees, regardless of their condition.

The tree-by-tree survey saved several ashes, and by the time it was over, Pepper says, "something had clicked inside of me. I realized that these forestry people needed help." Shortly after beginning his campaign, Pepper had learned that there were a handful of not-for-profit groups around the country that sponsored public tree plantings and tree stewardship. Putting his journalistic training to use, he called these organizations and the American Forestry Association. At a second meeting of the city Forestry Board, he stood up and spoke of these citizen-based initiatives and said, "Look, we need the same thing here."

Everyone agreed, and then a woman rose and told Pepper, "You're the one to do it." The speaker was Mary Pat Matheson, who has since served as president of the arboretum.

Pepper laughs. "I was flabbergasted. I had no intention of organizing this." He did, however, write an editorial for the *Tribune* calling for a "white knight" to step forward and form an organization similar to Minnesota's Twin Cities Tree Trust and the Los Angeles–based Tree-People.

And what was the public's response? One law firm sent a check for $75. "That was it," says Pepper. "I was devastated."

But not deterred. Intrigued by the fledgling citizen forestry movement, Pepper did more homework. Disease and urban sprawl were causing the removal of trees in Salt Lake City and other urban areas across the state and nation at an alarming rate, and owing to funding and manpower shortages, local governments were not replacing the trees.

The cement and blacktop that were replacing ashes and elms did not improve the economic or ecologic life of the city. In contrast, trees beautified areas, making commercial districts more consumer-friendly and enhancing property values in residential areas. They purified air and water, preventing runoff and absorbing particulates. And perhaps most important, Pepper learned in his conversations with conservationists, the simple act of planting trees can bring together a neighborhood or community. "Who can argue with this?" Pepper asks. "It's the ideal noncontroversial volunteer activity that can unite young and old, rich and poor, black and white, and once it's done you have a legacy that you and your children can watch grow "

While no one disputed such reasoning, the days passed without a white knight riding forward. Pepper finally realized that he indeed was the one to do it. He started slowly.

His first step was to learn more about the activities of the existing tree-planting groups. "There was no sense in reinventing the wheel," he explains. Some groups organized annual tree-planting events and raised money from individuals and corporations to support such activities. Some groups relied on membership drives to generate funds as well as a body of willing volunteers. Pepper found each approach appealing. "I felt a hybrid of the programs that already existed was best." Because he wanted the Utah initiative to last well into the future, he felt it was most important to have at least one annual event that could become a tradition. He also felt that an educational component was essential.

Although planting trees might seem a bit countercultural to some, Pepper thought that the organization should be modeled on successful businesses. This meant instituting strict accounting practices, relying on legal advisers to create a viable structure, and employing professional marketing and advertising techniques to promote the effort. Pepper hoped that experts would donate their services.

The board of directors of the organization would also be important. Having always envisioned the group as a community alliance, Pepper wanted corporate, government, and citizen representatives. Board members who were prominent and well respected he reasoned, would lend instant credibility to the effort.

Pepper thus began to make exploratory calls to citizens and businesses whose political and financial aid he would need in the future. He didn't promise these potential allies a rose garden . . . or a forest. "I merely said, 'If I were to do this, would you help?' " Among those saying yes were a local tree nursery, which later gave discounts; an ad agency, which later donated its services; state forestry officials, who were willing to participate in plantings; and Pepper's employer, the *Tribune,* which provided editorial and financial support. The *Tribune's* law firm also contributed its services. By invoking the names of prominent individuals and representatives of institutions willing to serve on a steering board, Pepper was able to enlist others in the effort. Former governor Calvin Rampton, who had sponsored a tree planting during his time in office, agreed to chair the organization, providing the credibility the effort needed.

Pepper acknowledges that his energy and enthusiasm were essential in building the public mandate for the program, but he downplays his salesmanship. "Let's face it. I had that rare, perfect concept that everyone could support. Who's going to argue with the idea of planting trees?" Particularly when presented with compelling evidence about the benefits.

Pepper gathered some impressive statistics. Two million trees, he noted, can remove four hundred tons of dust and smoke from the air each day. And over a fifty-year lifetime, a tree generates $31,250 worth of oxygen, provides $62,000 worth of air pollution control, recycles $37,000 worth of water, and controls $31,250 of soil erosion.

Pepper wanted to announce the creation of TreeUtah with a bang. An Arbor Day ceremony at a new city/county building seemed the perfect time. When Salt Lake City's mayor, Palmer DePaulis, asked Pepper for help with a speech germane to the occasion, Pepper asked if the mayor would introduce TreeUtah to the media and citizenry. And thus on April 28, 1989, some two years after Pepper's epiphany, TreeUtah was officially born.

In keeping with Pepper's "big event" philosophy, the organization hit the ground running with a Founders' Planting. About thirty people instrumental in creating TreeUtah planted sixty-two ten- to fifteen-foot trees at Pioneer Trail State Park, on the city's outskirts. These individuals or the organizations with which they were affiliated paid for the trees —$175 apiece.

Today, families, scouts, schools, neighborhood groups, community organizations, and individual citizens plant seedlings and trees, which they purchase themselves or with corporate support, usually at a discount from participating nurseries. Other big annual events, like Plant a Family Tree Week and the April Run Through the Trees, have also become traditions, attracting thousands of citizens. And when fires and other natural disasters destroy the state's forests, TreeUtah volunteers participate in reforestation.

In addition to the *Tribune,* Utah Power and its parent corporation, PacifiCorp, have provided considerable support. Trees, after all, reduce energy costs and pollution. Pepper describes the involvement of a coal-burning company at such a grass-roots environmental level as a breakthrough.

TreeUtah expects to have planted 100,000 trees by 1996. The budget is currently $200,000 a year, and two full-time paid staff members were hired in 1992. This growth is most satisfying to Pepper, who insists he was always confident, despite the frustration and loneliness during the early days, when responsibility fell on him to start the organization. "People say, 'I'll bet you never expected it would grow so big, so fast.' But I honestly tell them I always knew it would."

The ash trees still remain in Pepper's front yard. Not too long ago, Pepper and his wife and young children planted a cherry tree in their back yard during Plant a Family Tree Week. "I know that tree will be around long after I'm gone," Pepper says. "That's what this is all about —having a hand in creating a legacy. I can't tell you how wonderful it is to feel so passionately about something that can do such good."

To contact TreeUtah, write to
TreeUtah,
P.O. Box 11506, Salt Lake City, UT 84147-0506.
Phone: 801-363-5900.

Pickup Games

TRENT AND TODD GYORY AND COURTNEY AND BRIAN GUERRIERI

> **The program:** Four children started a recycling program in their community, which did not offer the service. They picked up glass, aluminum, some plastic, and tin cans from approximately fifty households. They then sorted, cleaned, repackaged, and delivered the materials to a recycling site in the area.

On a warm spring afternoon not too long after Earth Day 1990, some seventy families in Herminie, Pennsylvania, opened their doors and mailboxes to find a simple flier that asked a straightforward question: Are you willing to help the community by recycling? The fliers had been delivered by four St. Edward's School students on bicycle and foot. Courtney Guerrieri was thirteen years old. Her brother, Brian, was nine. Their friends Todd and Trent Gyory were eight and eleven years old, respectively.

Many municipalities across America do not have recycling programs. When the Guerrieris and Gyorys began their campaign, Pennsylvania did not require townships with fewer than five thousand people to provide such services. Thus, Sewickley Township, a rural community of two thousand about an hour from Pittsburgh, did not offer curbside pickup of recyclable materials. Environmentally conscious citizens in the township had two choices: they could either sort their own bottles and cans and drop them off at a site in Greensburg, about fifteen miles away, or they could continue to throw their bottles and cans in the regular trash and hope for recycling to be mandated in their community.

But Courtney, Brian, Todd, and Trent offered a third choice. The students were willing to start a recycling program in their neighborhood. Residents had only to leave the appropriate materials by their doors one day a week. The youngsters would do the rest—collect it, sort it, repackage it, and deliver it to a recycling center in Greensburg—at no charge.

Most kids would rather spend their spare time playing pickup games than picking up trash, or sorting through baseball cards instead of sorting cans and bottles. What motivated these youngsters to act? Trent explains that the quartet had long been concerned about the environment, thanks in part to an inspiring teacher, Donna Blasi. Todd, who was in third grade when they began, adds, "I've always been fanatic about the environment. I've been a member of Greenpeace for a long time." Courtney had lobbied her parents to shop responsibly by avoiding aerosol cans, Styrofoam plates, and other environmentally damaging products. And Brian had been "radicalized" when he saw a duck with the plastic from a six-pack around its neck.

Earth Day 1990 provided the impetus for action. Trent was working on a school project about pollution when his mother, Barb, suggested that the students initiate a small-scale recycling effort. "I thought, maybe we can't control the rest of the world, but by golly, we can control our home," she recalls. She confesses that she envisioned her sons taking a wagon within a few blocks of their home to collect their neighbors' bottles and cans during summer vacation. The kids, however, had bigger plans—an effort that would cover a three- to four-mile radius and last beyond the summer.

The Gyorys called their friends the Guerrieris, who were equally enthusiastic. The foursome began by seeking and gaining the permission of the local Sanitation Department to start a volunteer recycling program. They then designed and distributed a simple one-page flier notifying neighbors of their free service; they would pick up recyclables every Tuesday. Obviously, parental participation would be essential if the anticipated demand materialized. A car or truck would be necessary for both pickup and delivery to Greensburg. Barb and Dennis Gyory and David and Susan Guerrieri agreed to drive and supervise.

About twenty-five households signed on initially. Pickup began about three weeks after the flier was distributed. As word of the service spread, the number of households doubled. The young environmentalists were collecting well over two hundred pounds a week.

The volunteer effort was a two-family affair. Each Tuesday evening the youngsters and one or more of their parents would drive the collection route in a pickup truck, stopping at each participating home. They would then bring the materials back to their own garages. On Saturdays they would sort the materials by type and color, remove labels from cans, repackage everything, and drive it to Greensburg. Eventually, two trucks were needed. Pickup took less than an hour, but the Saturday sorting and delivery took three to four hours. Each Saturday after the work was done, the parents would take the kids out for a special lunch.

Courtney, Brian, Todd, and Trent did receive a few dollars a month from the recycling facility in payment for the aluminum cans they delivered. Such payment, however, amounted to less than a dollar per hour of work and did not even cover the expense of gas and Saturday lunch. But the motivation was not monetary. "We just wanted to remind people that the little bags collected can add up to make a big difference on the earth," Todd says.

Todd and his partners admit that despite their noble goal, the work was often tedious and difficult, particularly during the winter. Brian told a local newspaper, "Sometimes we get angry and don't want to do it, but we still do it for Mother Earth." Peeling labels and sorting trash into thirty or more bags in an unheated garage on a cold Saturday instead of going to a movie or the mall requires tremendous commitment. Barb Gyory notes that while she doesn't hold a great deal of hope that adults will see the light—she hopes it won't be through a hole in the ozone layer—she is encouraged by the effort of schoolchildren like hers and the Guerrieris'.

In partial defense of adults, it should be noted that Sewickley Township eventually instituted a formal recycling program. After more than a year as the only mass recyclers in town, the Gyorys and Guerrieris were no longer needed. Although they were delighted that recycling would take place on an even larger scale, the youngsters greeted the news with mixed emotions. "A lot of kids asked us why we were wasting our time, but I liked doing it. I liked helping the earth," says Trent. "I think the people who made fun of us were mostly jealous. I felt sad to give it up."

For further information, contact
Trent and Todd Gyory,
109 McClerge, Herminie, PA 15637;
and Courtney and Brian Guerrieri,
2 Brian Drive, Herminie, PA 15637.

The Pathfinder

ANNE LUSK AND THE STOWE RECREATION PATH

The program: With some government support and private donations large and small, a rural community planned and built a 5.3-mile public recreation path, or greenway, on land that is almost exclusively privately owned. The greenway—eight feet of asphalt flanked by grass—not only affords a new perspective on the local scenery, it serves as a shared space, a common ground for townspeople and tourists of all ages and backgrounds on foot, on bikes, on skates, on skis, in baby strollers, and in wheelchairs.

Anne Lusk, the force behind the Stowe (Vermont) Recreation Path and the guru of America's grass-roots greenway movement, wishes she could visit your community to sell you what she calls a "natural sidewalk" or "linear park." She wishes she could roll out a carpet of greenway for you and say, "Try it for a month. If you don't like it, I'll take it back." She's confident that there will be no returns—that you and your fellow citizens will see that these recreational paths can rejuvenate your community.

Listen to her pitch: "These paths would be for walking, biking, cross-country skiing, or watching wildlife. And unlike town sidewalks built by the edge of the road, greenways can run along a riverbank, head into the country, and then scoot back into town. They can be placed on the edge of a field where the farmer never mows, or they can go to and from and through the town's parks.

"A well-placed greenway gives people a way to get around town without using a car. Kids can ride their bikes to the ballpark or home after school and not have to be cautioned about Main Street traffic. People can use a greenway for everyday recreation. It's an alternative for people who want to exercise and enjoy their free time. And last, but perhaps best, the path gives back to a town a place where people can engage in that neighborly 'porch-swing' socializing, a location for those general store–type benches and places for kids to hang out."

Visit the Stowe Recreation Path on a summer's day and Anne's words about the 5.3-mile greenway come alive. There are indeed townsfolk and tourists of all ages jogging and walking and using all modes of transportation save one. There are bikes, rollerblades, strollers, wheelchairs, but no cars.

Some people on the greenway move with purpose. Others meander, just as the path does. Some stop altogether to sit on the benches and enjoy each other's company and the scenery. Mount Mansfield is a star attraction of the path, but so too is the West Branch River. The path crisscrosses the river on cambered wood-floored bridges.

Although not all communities can compete with Stowe in scenery, Anne firmly believes that all communities can and should have their own greenways. In urban settings, greenways might be built along abandoned railroad tracks, for example. Use, not beauty, is the principal goal, she says.

Anne is not alone in championing the "greenwaying" of America. In 1987, the President's Commission on the Outdoors heartily endorsed the concept and encouraged communities to build these conservation, transportation, and recreation corridors. Of course, by that time Stowe was six years into creating its path.

The path was the brainchild of a local resident, Claire Lintillhac. Concerned about safety on the roads, Ms. Lintillhac in 1977 commissioned the Vermont Highway Department to design a local bike route. The department ruled out a path along the shoulder of the existing farm road leading to Mount Mansfield and instead designed a separate but parallel route. But the plans gathered dust until 1981, when the Stowe Area Commission, the equivalent of the local Chamber of Commerce, resurrected the idea. The commission allocated $10,000 to hire a bike/walk administrator for two years. Duties included supervising path design, raising funds, coordinating publicity, and securing deeds of easement from private property owners whose land would be needed for the path.

Anne admits that she was somewhat hesitant to apply for the position. She had no direct experience in this field. A former art student and model in New York, she had come to Stowe in 1971 to become, in her words, "a ski bum." She then married a local ski patrolman, earned a master's degree in historic preservation from the University of Vermont, and led a volunteer effort that successfully restored a nineteenth-century hall to become the town library. The others applying for the position—all men—seemed to have considerably more experience in civic affairs; one went on to become the mayor of the largest city in Vermont.

Anne's reservations about her qualifications were, however, dwarfed by her reservations about the feasibility of the project. The town had no history of bike paths. There wasn't enough money for a path. And, most daunting, there was no land immediately available for the path. More than two dozen property owners had parcels where the path was designed to go. Since Stowe couldn't afford to buy their land, and, as Anne notes, "eminent domain and condemnation are unspeakable in a small town," the administrator would have to persuade the property owners to *give* small portions of their land to Stowe.

Still, the project excited and challenged Anne, who was riding high from her successful renovation project. She applied for and was given the job. "They knew they'd get their money's worth from me," she says with a smile.

Anne felt no pressure to begin construction overnight. She moved deliberately. "The first year was fact-finding and building community support," she says. "The second year was raising money and securing deeds of easement." Work on the path itself did not begin until year three.

As she is now recognized as one of the nation's authorities on building greenways, Anne should be a primary source for anyone or any community interested in such a project. The path she followed is instructive. "I knew nothing about building a greenway, so the first order of business was to educate myself." She immediately read every booklet or path "how-to" she could find.

Having educated herself, she began educating the rest of the town. During her first year as administrator, she wrote a steady stream of articles about recreational paths for the local newspaper. "These became the foundation for working with the community," she says.

But her contact with the community involved far more than writing articles. "Building a greenway is a collaborative effort. I wanted as much input from others as possible." She enlisted several people in town to serve as her sounding boards and mentors. "They were handpicked, either to represent a broad constituency or because they always had good ideas," she says. She also spoke regularly to high school classes, the Rotary Club, the women's club, church groups, and elementary schoolchildren.

As enthusiasm and support for the project grew in town, Anne began to approach property owners. "They needed to be assured that their land was theirs and if a path was to be built, it would be their idea. Rather than showing up with a pre–Magic Markered map, I approached the property owners with blank maps and pencils. Together we would start connecting the dots." This was a lengthy process and required much give-and-take, for property owners were justifiably wary of giving away portions of their land—even the least desirable portions. Because the owners requested only quiet users, the deeds excluded any motorized vehicles.

The path's route met all the recommendations for an ideal greenway. Says Anne, "It combines sun and shade, hills and flat, open fields and arbored canopies, straight stretches and meandering curves, views of a mountain, and a companion river with a swimming hole." An outsider comes away with the feeling that Anne's charm, energy, and perseverance were instrumental in gaining both community and property owner support. Anne offers an additional explanation: gender. "I think women are by nature consensus builders. I know I am."

The deeds Anne secured would not be valid unless the money was raised to build what had been christened the Stowe Recreation Path. The engineers hired to prepare the plans estimated that the first, 2.7-mile stretch would cost $300,000 and the final 2.6 miles, $380,000. "Compared to obtaining the land, raising the money was easier and more fun," says Anne. Again she tried to involve the entire community. Ms. Lintillhac made a sizable contribution, but the path could not have been built without the small donations of individuals, who purchased lengths of the path at $2 per inch, $45 per yard, and $250 per rod. A silent auction and black-tie dinner-dance with Peter Duchin's orchestra, free champagne and truffles, and appearances by three governors, a state representative, actress Deborah Raffin, and Dr. Ruth raised $40,000. The federal government provided the remaining $160,000, some from general revenue-sharing funds and most from the Interior Department's Land and Water Conservation Fund.

Anne now consults with other communities interested in recreation paths and is also a familiar figure in the offices of the Interior Department and the halls of Congress as she presses for greater national support of local greenways. Both she and the town of Stowe have received numerous national awards for their work on the path, and when she speaks, legislators and members of the executive branch listen. But her greatest reward comes from seeing the path in use. "There's a humbling satisfaction in having helped create a greenway in a small town," she says. "Every day you see the townspeople who helped make it happen, and you see so many who enjoy the finished path. Building a greenway is something an American community can actually do and, once completed, use with pride."

For further information, contact
Anne Lusk,
1531 River Road, Stowe, VT 05672.
Phone: 802-253-7758.

4.
NEIGHBORHOOD SAFETY

Street Smarts

JOHN FOSTER AND M.A.D. D.A.D.S.

The program: Caring men serve as parental role models and address issues concerning youth. They raise public awareness about drug abuse, strengthen the family unit, and address community apathy over crime and youth violence. They counsel youngsters. In organized patrols, they are a comforting presence on the streets, in the projects, at school functions, and at other public places and events. They come face to face with drug dealers, drug addicts, and gang members, challenging their activities and providing referral services.

John Foster is not the kind of dad that you want to make mad. Witness the events that inspired the Omaha, Nebraska, father of six to create Men Against Destruction—Defending Against Drugs and Social-disorder, or M.A.D. D.A.D.S. for short. In the spring of 1989, John was awakened late one night by the horrifying entrance of his twenty-year-old son, Sean, beaten and bloody. Between labored breaths, Sean told him that five young men had attacked him at a north Omaha gas station and tried to steal his brand-new Suzuki Samurai. They apparently liked the vehicle's colors.

Having just returned from a church group outing in North Carolina, John was particularly full of love for his fellow man. He was thankful that Sean was not seriously injured and would recover, and that the attackers had not been able to wrest the Samurai from him. But anger fueled by paternal instinct overruled his strong Christian feelings.

"I lost control when I saw my son like that," he admits. This is a frightening thought. Standing six feet five inches tall and weighing 271 pounds, the fifty-year-old union official strikes a commanding presence when he is *not* angry.

In his rage John found his two guns, put them on the front seat of his car, and sped off in search of the five thugs, who were driving what Sean thought was a brown 1978 Monte Carlo. "I stopped people on the street," he remembers. "I went to the bowling alley and the housing projects. Nothing. So I parked by the corner of Twenty-ninth and Patrick, where the gangs hang out. I stood by the side of my car, waiting. And I realized I was just a *mad dad.* I told myself that we had to do something about all this violence, about all these lost kids. We had to get men organized and take on the problem."

John returned home empty-handed, but with a head full of ideas. He had concluded that it was less important to find those who had attacked Sean that evening than it was to find a way to deal with the daily destruction and disorder in the community. Innocent people were being victimized. They deserved safe streets. The offenders had to be brought to justice, but they also had to be helped. And future drug dealers and gang members had to be shown that there was an alternative to a life of crime, that education was the key to success and survival.

But how could these objectives be accomplished? John wasn't sure, but he didn't let his uncertainty prevent him from moving forward. He and his wife quickly put together five hundred fliers calling for a meeting of concerned men. Why limit it to men? Says John, "Women have a tremendous amount to give. They've always been aggressive and outfront when it comes to the problems of the young, particularly in the black community. But I knew from growing up myself that the youngsters were most likely to respect and respond to strong men of authority."

Within days of the attack on Sean, the Fosters distributed the fliers at a community forum on violence. When only five or six men showed up at the meeting John had organized, he realized he actively had to seek out committed, thoughtful, experienced kindred spirits. Over the next two weeks, he spoke with Eddie Staton, a former director of Omaha's Human Relations Commission; Dr. George Garrison, chair of black studies at the University of Nebraska at Omaha; and the Reverend Robert Tyler. Each signed on to address the problems John had identified. "It was a miracle that we all came together," says John.

Meeting for several evenings a week, this core group soon developed an outline for a grass-roots community organization to be called M.A.D. D.A.D.S. Dr. Garrison then wrote a detailed document explaining the program to potential members and to the community at large. "We want to work with any agency, organization, group, or individuals who are concerned about the future of our families," the paper began. "The very value of life itself has significantly declined in Black and other minority communities across the nation. This has resulted in conditions that leave residents both disadvantaged and living their lives in constant fear. . . . It is too late to deny that we are engaged in a WAR in the streets of America. We are not at war with our own youth, but with what our own youth are doing."

The document's "call to action" urged concerned fathers to help "organize our neighborhoods and become more visible and active participants with our children and our community." The plan followed. Mad dads would serve as surrogate fathers and big brothers, counsel and protect youth, tutor youngsters and assist them in getting job training and employment, identify and report to law enforcement agencies any criminals and the location of criminal activities, and provide a presence at community events.

At Dr. Tyler's invitation, John explained this plan to an alliance of Omaha ministers. "There was a lot of applause, and then someone asked if we were going to be a vigilante group," John recalls. "I said, 'No, we're coming together as concerned fathers. We will be more like chaperons.' " Members would not carry weapons; they would patrol the streets controlled by gangs and addicts, and appear at places and functions where innocent citizens might be victimized. They might very well confront criminals, but only with words, not with physical force.

The founders elected a board of directors and officers, installing John as president. In August 1989, less than four months after one mad dad had been moved to take action, M.A.D. D.A.D.S. was a reality.

John and the board's first task was to recruit fellow mad dads. They hoped to enlist fifty to seventy-five African American men to take turns patrolling the streets and providing other services in the community. To find these would-be volunteers, they contacted churches and schools and called their friends. Wisely, they also made certain that their first project would attract media attention and spread the word to all of Omaha.

Painting over gang graffiti was sure to win community support and television time. The founders persuaded a local paint store to donate supplies, identified buildings and other structures defaced by neighborhood gangs, alerted the television stations and newspapers about their goal for the day and the future, and proceeded to paint the town. "The young gang members didn't like us invading their turf, but the local news jumped on it," John recalls, smiling. By summer's end, about seventy-five men had enlisted.

Cleaning up a wall in daylight is different from cleaning up the streets after midnight. Initially, John and Eddie Staton constituted the entire patrol group. Each weekend the devoted pair would target streetcorners or local establishments where as many as three hundred kids between the ages of fourteen and twenty-two hung out into the wee hours of the morning. "It was mind-boggling at first," says John. "Not knowing what to expect, we just played it by ear We weren't there to provoke or intimidate but to extend our hands. We said, 'We're fathers, and we're here to help.' " Conversation took precedence over confrontation whenever possible.

Not everyone they encountered needed or wanted help, but some did. Those who told John and Eddie that they were looking for work, drug treatment, or a way out of the gang life were referred to individuals, centers, or social service agencies with the resources to provide assistance.

Gradually more men joined the patrols. These volunteers received training before donning the green-and-black T-shirts and caps that identified them as mad dads. The founders stressed that they were not to put themselves or others in harm's way; they were not to take on the role of police or interfere with law enforcement officers. They were to chaperon and counsel where appropriate.

Says John, "Just by being out there, we prevented crime from taking place. We were also able to diffuse some potentially explosive situations between the kids and the police." Not surprisingly, many of the young men and women in the projects or on the corners did not trust the cops Often John, Eddie, or other volunteers were able to serve as calming influences for both the police and the young people.

Having established a positive presence in the neighborhoods, the members of M.A.D. D.A.D.S. were asked to show up at community functions where trouble often occurred—school events, picnics, music concerts, and rallies. "We were happy to go, but again we stressed that we were chaperons, not security guards," says John. If called, the men in black and green—the black symbolic of unity, the green symbolic of life, growth, and hope—will also escort students fearful of gang violence.

Escort, chaperon, or patrol—whatever the mad dads do, it is clear they work in high-risk areas. This observation did not escape John's family, who at first feared for his safety and did not support his efforts.

John acknowledges that there have been some dicey moments on the street. On one occasion he arrived at a grocery store to find a young man contemplating how to deal with a group of toughs waiting for him outside. The boy showed John a gun and said, "Mr. Foster, if they mess with me, I'm going to lullaby them." John persuaded the boy to turn over the weapon, then walked him through the angry crowd to a car. "The kids on the street were mad at me. But I got him out safely," he says.

Members of M.A.D. D.A.D.S. make it a point to give out their phone numbers. On another occasion, John received a call from a fifteen-year-old high school dropout who needed $200 to pay off the crack dealer for whom he worked. The boy had mistakenly given a customer credit. The customer had disappeared and now the dealer wanted the cash. John initially refused to pay off the debt. "I despise drug dealers," he says emphatically. But he finally gave the boy the money out of his own pocket. "He was so appreciative. He told me he was able to sleep for the first time in weeks." John continued to work with the boy, who quit the drug business, returned to high school, and then entered the military.

Success stories like these eventually converted John's wife and children to the cause. Others, too, have been impressed. At last count Omaha boasted about nine hundred mad dads. The youngsters they assist are black and white, rich and poor. Recognizing that all citizens can help this diverse population in some way, the group does not discriminate on the basis of gender or race. Ten percent of the members are women, and whites account for about three quarters of the organization. About 150 of the members serve on the street patrols. Others provide support services by printing fliers and raising funds. And many participate in the organization's rapidly growing community outreach and educational programs.

M.A.D. D.A.D.S.' most recent annual report notes that in addition to speaking to thousands of community residents on the streets, members made more than four hundred presentations to schools, spoke at more than five hundred service club functions, visited more than three hundred churches, and spoke at three hundred dinner, lunch, or breakfast gatherings. Thanks to funds raised at a softball benefit held in conjunction with the local Fox television network affiliate, the organization teamed with the Urban League of Nebraska to publish a pamphlet to show parents how to get involved in their children's schools.

M.A.D. D.A.D.S.' achievements in Omaha have triggered inquiries from concerned citizens in several other cities. "M.A.D. D.A.D.S. will work anywhere in the country where there are strong, drug-free men," says Eddie Staton. Chapters are now operating in Houston, Denver, New York, Baltimore, and several smaller cities.

Eddie, Dr. Tyler, and John Foster enthusiastically share their experiences and insights with those who might want to start a chapter in their community. "This is not a program, it's a movement," says John. "We're not the answer, but a piece of the puzzle that can work. We can provide the script, but you have to provide the players. You must be in it for the long haul. We are."

> For further information about M.A.D. D.A.D.S., contact John Foster or Eddie Staton at 2221 North 24th Street, Omaha, NE 68110.

Kid Power

LINDA WARSAW-CHAMPIN AND KIDS AGAINST CRIME

> **The program:** Young volunteers help schoolchildren learn to avoid abuse and criminal victimization through educational programs and community involvement. The organization also

offers teens an alternative to joining gangs and committing crimes.

The burglar had ransacked the entire home, emptying cupboards, throwing drawers on the floor. "He had gone through *my possessions*," recalls Linda Warsaw-Champin, who was ten when the burglary occurred in 1985. "I felt violated, and I felt helpless."

Fortunately for children across the country, Linda was eventually able to overcome her feeling of helplessness and fight back. Two years after the burglary, she organized a group of friends and classmates in San Bernardino, California, to form Kids Against Crime (KAC). Today, KAC is recognized as America's preeminent youth-run anticrime organization. In 1992 alone, the organization's 4,700 school-age members reached an audience of more than 22,500 children. These volunteer crime-stoppers counseled and referred three thousand peers who utilized the Kids Against Crime telephone hotline, made more than fifty school presentations about crime and abuse, conducted sixty separate graffiti cleanups, and fingerprinted 1,771 children. Law enforcement authorities utilize these fingerprints when children are abducted.

In college now and pushing twenty-one, Linda admits that she is amazed at the growth and success of the initiative. "It's hard to believe, but everything I dreamed of when I first conceived of Kids Against Crime has become a reality."

After the burglary, Linda was afraid to enter her house alone. She could not sleep. How did KAC grow from such helplessness?

Linda credits her mother, Nellie, with helping her overcome her fears by suggesting that the two of them volunteer to work in a victim's assistance program organized by the local district attorney. Working after school in the courthouse, Linda heard about cases involving children who had been abused. Shocked to learn that most of the victims knew and trusted their attackers, she asked permission to sit in on cases, just to make sure that these stories of abuse by friends and even relatives were true.

After hearing an eight-year-old girl painfully describe being molested by her babysitter, Linda cried. "I have to do something," she told Nellie. "Kids need to be educated so they aren't abused by the people they love and trust."

The fact that she was still a kid herself did not deter her from taking action. "So what if I'm not eighteen and can't vote," she said to herself. "So what if I'm smaller. I can make a difference."

At home that night, she wrote down ideas for an organization run by kids that would help stop the abuse of children. Her wish list included school workshops that focused on how to prevent abuse and report criminal conduct and a telephone hotline staffed by trained young people. After completing the list, she identified those adults who could help her refine and implement her plan. "I typed up my proposal and took it to District Attorney Dennis Kottmier and other city officials," she recalls. These included the mayor, the chief of police, and others dealing with abused children. Everyone she approached was supportive, and D.A. Kottmier was so impressed that he offered Linda office space.

With city officials behind her, Linda was ready to approach her peers. She announced her intentions to a group of friends from school and the neighborhood and invited them to a meeting at her house. About twenty young people attended. "I can make a difference" had become "We can make a difference."

Linda was not interested in being a dictator. "I wanted the input of all my friends," she says. The group decided to concentrate on developing a speakers program that would bring experts on a variety of crime-related topics into the schools. School officials responded to this idea enthusiastically, and over the first year several speakers from the law enforcement community participated.

Because young children have the most difficulty resisting and reporting abuse and other criminal activity, they are the primary audience for Kids Against Crime. They are not, however, an ideal audience for listening to serious speeches. Linda and her group talked with child specialists and decided that skits offered the best way to get a message across to the little ones. Assisted by professionals from city government, the school system, and social service agencies, the young volunteers of KAC developed and presented short plays about child abuse and the danger of drugs. The professionals also helped design workshops for older children on these subjects as well as rape, teen pregnancy, and AIDS

These hot issues are also among the many topics of conversation on

KAC's telephone hotline. Thirty-six young people supervised by twelve adults handle calls, providing sympathetic ears and referrals to appropriate social service agencies. Linda stresses that KAC volunteers receive extensive training before participating in any activities, particularly the hotline, where those interested in fielding calls must first attend twenty-four hours of workshops held by representatives from various networking agencies.

How does KAC attract volunteers? Chapters established in schools are a primary recruiting vehicle. Graffiti cleanups and fingerprinting booths create a presence in the community and also bring in new members. And media coverage helps spread the word. "The newspapers, magazines, and television have been interested in us from the beginning," says Linda. An article in *National Geographic World,* a magazine for children, attracted 350 members. A feature on CNN recently elicited a call from a gentleman interested in starting a chapter in Colorado. And another television story moved a district attorney in Pennsylvania to initiate the same program.

As members pay no dues, KAC depends on outside funding to support its programs and administration, which now includes three paid employees. Grants from the city of San Bernardino, local service clubs, corporations, and foundations supply the $100,000 needed to operate each year. Linda confesses that neither she nor her mother, who has helped administer KAC from the beginning, knew anything about grant writing, so her mother took a course in the subject. The course has paid off. In addition to competing successfully for corporate funds, KAC has recently been awarded the services of VISTA volunteers, who are trained to assist grass-roots community organizations.

Linda, who is majoring in business so that she can continue to make KAC a professional group, hopes these VISTA volunteers can help expand the organization. She cites statistics about the growing number of young people who are victimized each year and the growing number of young people who commit crimes. Convinced that KAC can both empower children to protect themselves and dissuade teens from engaging in antisocial activity, she now has a new dream: "I hope for the day when we have a chapter helping kids in every school in the country."

For further information, contact
Linda Warsaw-Champin, Kids Against Crime,
P.O. Box 22004, San Bernardino, CA 92406.
The KAC hotline, in service twenty-four hours a day on weekends
and after school on weekdays, is 1-800-KAC-5670.

Guns and Roses

EDITH HENRY AND THE LAFITTE
BEAUTIFICATION AND GARDEN CLUB

> **The program:** Housing project residents form a garden club to beautify their surroundings, promote neighborhood pride, and discourage criminal activity.

Edith Henry joyfully rattles off the names of the weapons that she and the other women in her New Orleans neighborhood have used to kick out the drug dealers and silence the gunfire that used to ring out in front of their homes. Everything in her arsenal, she notes, was purchased over the counter at the local K mart or Home Depot, without the need for license, waiting period, or criminal background check "We've got rosebushes, hibiscus, crape myrtles, snapdragons, and sweet potatoes, to name a few," she says.

How has such flora weeded out the criminals who once shot their guns and dealt their drugs on Edith's block in the mammoth Lafitte housing development, a ten-minute bus ride from Bourbon Street? "The gang members and drug dealers say, 'Let's stay out of this area. It's too clean,'" explains Edith, a sixty-year-old retired housekeeper.

When Edith moved to Lafitte from Baton Rouge in 1980, she found that in the project, cleanliness was not next to godliness, it was next to impossible Few residents seemed to take pride in the property surrounding their low-rise units, she says. And Edith understood why As public housing tenants, they felt no sense of ownership in their apartments or small yards and thus no urge to beautify them. The government's inability to maintain the area added to this sense of disenfranchisement. One sad result of this neighborhood indifference was that criminals felt right at home. The unkept lawns, sidewalks, and streets provided fertile territory for conducting gang business.

Having been taught as a young child to care for her surroundings, Edith's idea of letting a neighborhood go to seed differed from that of most of her neighbors in Lafitte. Shortly after moving in, she planted a garden. Her aim at this time was not to combat crime but simply to beautify her world. Two neighbors, Delores Wood and Etheline DeJean, shared this sensibility—and the community's derision over their gardening in front of their units. "Oh, for a long time a lot of the people laughed at us out there digging holes," remembers Edith.

After several years of planting flowers and shrubs in their own yards, the three kindred spirits decided they wanted to plant a notion with their neighbors. "We needed to get across that it's important to keep things up where you live, whether it's in the projects or someplace else," Edith explains. And so in 1987 she and Delores and Etheline formed the Lafitte Beautification and Garden Club.

Neighbors were recruited with a sales pitch as soft as rose petals. "I know you're renting," Edith would say. "But nothing's impossible. All you have to do is make up your mind to try to change things." As proof she could point to the three mini-Edens on the block. Soon club membership totaled one dozen—all women, as it happened—and Galvez Street took on a very different look.

Of course, planting and maintaining gardens takes more than just green thumbs. Money was necessary to buy flowers, bushes, small trees, and tools such as shovels. When club members met on the third Saturday of each month, they each brought $2 in dues. They raised additional funds by collecting cans and cashing them in at a nearby recycling center.

Tending their gardens, club members tended to see more of what was happening on the streets than their neighbors. Aware that the projects were a ripe place for crime, Edith frequently flagged down police cars, introduced herself, and expressed her concerns about drug dealing and other illicit activity. Eventually she and other club members sought to beautify the neighborhood not only by adding gardens but by subtracting criminals. They formed a Neighborhood Watch group, which meets regularly with the police and monitors and reports suspicious behavior in the area.

Such behavior has decreased significantly in recent years, says Edith, thanks to the gardeners and a curious form of chivalry by the would-be drug dealers. "They may be criminals, but they still respect us for what we're doing in keeping up the neighborhood," explains Edith She adds that while these criminals find the neighborhood too clean for their dirty business, vigilance is still required to keep them away. "If someone up to no good parks on our block, I tell them just to keep going The other night a young man got out of his car and I said, 'Are you going to be here long?' He looked at me and my yard and said, 'I'm leaving now, mother,' and I said, 'Thank you and have a good evening'"

In recent years the club has expanded its efforts to make life more beautiful for those in the projects by playing Santa to needy children and providing food baskets to senior citizens. Again, dues and recycling money support these efforts. The club does not solicit contributions, and the only outside support has come from Texaco, which at the request of a local police officer donated fencing for the gardens (thus proving that good fences make good neighborhoods)

In 1993, Edith and her daughter moved to another unit in the project, several blocks away from their original apartment. Predictably, Edith quickly planted a garden. While maintaining her membership in the club, she also began persuading her new neighbors to form a new club "I'd like to see them spring up all over the project," she says "It's hard work to keep up a garden, but the results are beautiful." People have long since stopped laughing at her when she preaches this gospel. "They see the difference. Yes, indeed, Lord, they see the difference"

For further information, contact
Edith Henry, Lafitte Garden and Beautification Club,
4338 Paris Avenue, New Orleans, LA 70122.

5.
ARTS AND RECREATION

Film Exposure

SHEILA DIVOLA BERGMAN AND THE EDUCATION PROJECT

The program: An organization brings the film arts to disadvantaged young people by providing the opportunity to produce photography, independent film, and video. Hands-on training is offered through workshops at schools and shelters and through one-on-one projects with noted artists and filmmakers who volunteer their time.

After fifteen years of figuring out how best to bring the film arts to young people, Sheila Divola Bergman thinks she finally has an answer. "Pizza," says the director of the Education Project (TEP), her tongue only partly in cheek.

To prove her point, Sheila cites a recent free twelve-week workshop sponsored by the New York City–based TEP at Urban Family Center, one of the city's largest shelters for homeless families. Although TEP posted fliers at the center announcing the opportunity to learn about videomaking from established artists and to create personal video journals, only a couple of youngsters showed up at the first Saturday morning meeting. Sheila then "got on a bullhorn" to summon more participants. "Wake up and learn how to be the next Spike Lee," she called. When only a few more curious souls wandered in, Sheila took to the bullhorn again, this time offering free pizza to those who participated. Faster than a Domino's delivery, the workshop was filled.

Of course, artists and would-be artists do not live by food alone. A slice of pizza may have lured the youngsters to the workshop, but it was the opportunity to produce slice-of-life videos under the supervision of talented professionals that hooked them. Three months later, more than a dozen kids who had never before held camcorders proudly gave their journals a premiere for family, fellow shelter residents, and the New York film community. Each participant was given a videotape of his or her production, but they came away with more than just a cassette. "In my video, I could tell people what it's like to be me," said one fourteen-year-old boy. Sheila adds, "The workshop fostered self-esteem, and it reignited their interest in learning and self-expression."

Sheila has been involved in firing up children since working at a not-for-profit center for the arts in Boston several years ago. There she helped coordinate programs in which well-known performance artists worked with inner-city children Moving on to the Anthology Film Archive, a New York City museum with one of the world's largest collections of independent and avant-garde film, Sheila continued reaching out to kids.

While some of the older filmmakers who came to showings at the archive lamented that they were a dying breed, Sheila was convinced that a new generation of artists was currently being raised on MTV. Already familiar with the medium, these young people had only to be exposed to the opportunities for artistic and political expression in video and film.

With the blessing of archive director and filmmaker Jonas Mekas, Sheila instituted a new program designed to introduce teenagers to noncommercial film and video. Searching the archives, she found several films that would appeal to this audience, among them two remarkably well-done shorts produced by one of the creators of the Teenage Mutant Ninja Turtles when he was about ten years old.

Having yet to discover the power of pizza, Sheila employed more conventional means of drawing youngsters to the screenings. She invited schools, shelters for homeless families, and other agencies serving inner-city children to participate. Why the concentrated outreach to these young people? "The kids of middle-class America already get exposed to the film and video medium," Sheila explains. "Many of them have camcorders We needed to hear the voice of the disadvantaged." Sheila also thought that these children might better relate to the independent films of the 1950s and 1960s, many of which were "raw in a street sense "

Introducing these young people to film and video was only the first step in Sheila's master plan. Phase two involved giving them the opportunity to make their own art. Unfortunately, the archive did not have the resources to launch such a program. So in 1990, after brainstorming with Carolyn Grifel, a filmmaker interested in involving the disadvantaged in art, Sheila decided to create a new not-for-profit entity, the Education Project.

Sheila, who went unpaid for TEP's first two years, provided the start-up money out of her own bank account. But she knew that the organization could survive only with outside funding from individuals, corporations, and foundations. To begin with, raising such money was difficult. "It was Catch-22," she says. "The people I approached said the programs I was proposing sounded fantastic but that the Education Project didn't have a track record. But how were we going to get a track record if no one would fund our programs?"

Forced to find alternative sources of money, TEP contracted with Macy's to provide floor demonstrations about the power of video. Using camcorders from the electronics department, some of New York's foremost videomakers showed children the artistic possibilities of the medium. Were they successful? Says Sheila, "I actually still get letters from parents who tell me that their kids were turned on to video from these demonstrations."

Because the videomakers volunteered their services to TEP, the entire Macy's fee provided the funds to initiate a project aimed at children who rarely set foot in department stores. Sheila sent a written proposal for a video workshop to the director of the Urban Family Center. He gave her the go-ahead for the aforementioned project, at which she learned not only that youngsters responded to pizza but that they could produce moving documentaries when instructed by experienced video artists. Again, these artists donated their time, and in the middle of the project Panasonic donated eight camcorders that the young participants could use to chronicle their lives and their worlds.

A thirty-week film project at a New York City public school that allowed students to document the year was equally successful. Said one teacher, "The workshops taught our class how to relate to individual lives and the everyday world through the fine arts. My students have created projects about their school, community, and homes. These topics are just as important as reading, science, and math."

The school and shelter workshops have been repeated to similar acclaim. But it was a July 1993 exhibition that brought TEP national recognition and support to expand its programs. *Art Works—Teenagers and Artists Collaborate on Polaroid's 20 × 24 Camera* was a unique project that allowed ten at-risk teenagers to work one on one with some of the most vital contemporary artists in America.

The exhibition was conceived in 1992 by Janeil Englestad, who had recently become TEP's part-time program director. Wouldn't it be great if young people could work with established artists on Polaroid's five-foot-tall, 235-pound view camera? Janeil mused. There are only five such cameras in the world, but one is in a Polaroid studio in Soho. A conversation with the studio manager, John Reuter, and Polaroid executives resulted in the donation of studio time, which is normally billed at $1,000 a day. Recognized artists in the community, such as Chuck Close, Felix Gonzales-Torres, and William Wegman, agreed to participate

Equal attention was paid to selecting the teenagers. "They were chosen because they live in environments that present overwhelming challenges and obstacles," explains Sheila. "They are representatives of a much larger community of youth who are at risk of having little or no contact with the arts because they live in shelters, are overcoming drug addiction, and/or live in neighborhoods that have been devastated by unemployment and lack of public programs." TEP found the teens at the Urban Family Center and Odyssey House, a drug treatment facility. All had shown some interest and skill in the arts.

Each artist was paired with an adolescent. Close, for example, worked with an eighteen-year-old who was interested in symbols of strength and bravery. After considering several approaches, the pair eventually decided to superimpose an image of a lion on a portrait of the teenager Wegman helped an eighth-grader bring his graffiti murals to life.

The exhibition opened at the International Center for Photography in New York to rave reviews. After three months it started a two-year, seven-city tour TEP also published a sixty-page hardcover *Art Works* catalog, which it distributed free of charge to schools and libraries across the country

The success of the project brought forth artists and arts-minded corporations and foundations willing to work on and help fund other projects. *Art Works II,* for example, paired ten professional filmmakers with ten teenagers to create short films. Another program coupled twenty-five film/video artists and teenagers from around the city in a novel "shooting relay." Each pair documented its own perspective of the streets, passing a super-8 and 16mm camera to the next team after it filmed its designated section.

TEP hopes that such projects will not be one-shot deals. Teenagers who have participated in TEP programs are given the opportunity to continue working in the film/video or fine arts community through paid internships. The young men and women are placed in museums, non-profit organizations, corporations, or with individual artists. TEP holds a raffle to help pay for the internships.

TEP has also started a scholarship program, which will be supported by contributions and fees from particular projects. One such project gives teens and artists who have previously worked together the chance to reunite and design materials for the music and entertainment industries. Conversations between TEP and Polygram Records, for example, resulted in contracts to create two album covers. In return, Polygram helped fund scholarships for the participating teenagers. Sheila sees such revenue-generating projects as the wave of the future. "The traditional way of collecting foundation and individual contributions is a thing of the past," she says.

With TEP on relatively solid financial ground, Sheila and Janeil have recently received partial compensation for their work. But Sheila notes, "We both still have other part-time jobs to make ends meet." Sheila coordinates an arts program in a parochial school, while Janeil works for a not-for-profit wildlife organization.

Like others in this book, neither woman became involved in TEP because of the financial rewards. They are satisfied to count the number of young people whose lives have been changed by exposure to the arts. TEP touches more than 2,500 children a year, most of them in individual situations.

In recent years a handful of schools and not-for-profit organizations have also attempted to pair young people and established artists. In Chicago, an art teacher at an inner-city school matched her students with the city's top furniture designers to produce chairs that were both artistic and functional. The finished products were displayed at a gallery, and sales proceeds went to the youngsters.

Does one have to be an artist or a not-for-profit professional like Sheila to launch such an effort? No, says Sheila. She suggests that the perfect threesome to begin a program would include an educator, an artist, and "someone with lots of energy, just to keep everyone going."

Energetic souls interested in further information should contact Sheila Divola Bergman, The Education Project,
155 Avenue of the Americas, 14th Floor, New York, NY 10013.
Phone: 212-886-5447

The Art of the Deal

PHYLLIS ELLIS AND THE NOYES CULTURAL ARTS CENTER

The program: A small city turns an empty school building into a center for more than thirty artists. The artists receive reduced rent in return for performing community service.

Phyllis Ellis describes herself as the kind of woman people tend to avoid at cocktail parties. "They know I'm going to try to pick their pocket for something," she says. That something is almost always related to improving the artistic life of her Evanston, Illinois, community. For the past twenty-five years she has successfully raised money and consciousness to implement a number of innovative programs. Most notable is the Noyes Cultural Arts Center, which Phyllis conceived during a tour of an old Alexandria, Virginia, torpedo factory in the 1970s.

How did a one-time weapons facility inspire the creation of a home for artists? Phyllis explains that as a longtime lover of classical music, she had raised money for and served on the board of the Evanston Symphony Orchestra. Sensitive to the needs and aspirations of such institutions, she had organized the National Association of Urban and Community Symphony Orchestras. While in Washington, D C., for the group's first meeting, she and her husband learned of a city-owned center in nearby Alexandria where artists worked and performed in space rented for a reduced rate. Touring the center, they learned that it had formerly been a torpedo factory.

Phyllis's mind started racing. Evanston was already home to the Evanston Arts Center, a not-for-profit organization where a limited number of established artists could work, teach, and exhibit work. But the center did not have the space or financial resources to support the operation she envisioned. And while Evanston did not have any former munitions facilities, there had to be an abandoned or unused building suitable for the numerous established and new artists not affiliated with the center. Such a space would benefit the artists by providing afford-able rent and an environment where they could draw energy and inspi-ration from their peers. The general public would also benefit from a large, centralized place offering exhibitions, performances, and classes.

The excitement of this inspiration was tempered by the realization that implementation could not be accomplished overnight. How would such an undertaking be financed? And who would oversee its day-to-day operation?

Phyllis was already quite busy. In addition to her local and national symphony affiliations, she had started a school music program in Evans-ton. Initially, she had arranged for school performances by graduate student ensembles from Northwestern University. Then, when a local music teacher confronted her and insisted that children should not only hear music but play it, Phyllis led an effort that provided free instru-ments and instruction to underprivileged students.

Aware that she alone could not create a center for artists, Phyllis determined that Evanston should have an Arts Council, which could oversee this project as well as other arts-related initiatives. Such councils were beginning to spring up in many municipalities. Surely, she rea-soned, a progressive place like Evanston would support such a body. She approached then-mayor Edgar Vanneman and explained her idea, add-ing that other communities applied for state and federal grants through their arts councils.

The mayor was supportive, as were those in the arts and business communities whom Phyllis approached. To insure that the city's al-derpersons would pass legislation to create the Evanston Arts Council (EAC), Phyllis had one trick up her sleeve. "I brought a group of young Suzuki violin students to a public hearing and had them perform," she explains, laughing. In June 1975, the City Council established the EAC. Phyllis was appointed to the body and selected as its first chair.

From Phyllis's standpoint, the timing could not have been better. She had not found a suitable place for the artists' center she envisioned. Suddenly, however, a possible location emerged the old Noyes School.

Like many communities, Evanston had closed a number of schools because of low enrollment in the early 1970s Noyes was among them. Unlike some of the other buildings, Noyes held a special place in the hearts of Evanstonians. Both the original building, built in 1892, and a 1910 addition were typical of a style that, in the words of one architectural historian, "merged the blocky Italianate and Romanesque manner with a stripped classicism and careful brickwork to produce an august monumentality with a great economy of means "

The landmark had sat vacant for several years while citizens and city officials debated its use. Some suggested tearing the building down to create more open space; some argued that it should be replaced by public housing. The majority of Evanstonians, however, wanted to see the building preserved Most important, the school district, which still owned Noyes, wanted to keep the building in case student enrollment rose and it would be needed again. A recreation center was needed in this part of the city. However, neighborhood residents argued that locating it at Noyes would be too disruptive.

Opposition to a recreational center peaked just as the Arts Council began operations, and Phyllis and her fellow commissioners seized the moment Why not turn the school into a cultural center? the EAC suggested. The people opposing the recreational center indicated they would consider such a use. To persuade these residents and the entire community of the viability of an arts center, the EAC held public hearings. It also worked behind the scenes, trying to garner support from artists, businesspeople, and city officials. Phyllis remembers that the endorsement of the respected Evanston Arts Center was very helpful.

By the time the hearings concluded, Evanston's citizens and city officials supported the project After agreeing to purchase the building from the school district, the city directed Phyllis and her fellow commissioners to manage it as an arts center. Although the actual purchase did not take place until 1980, the EAC moved into the building immediately.

Word quickly spread through the arts community that space was available for rent at Noyes. Recognizing that artists often lead a financially unstable existence, the EAC determined that it would offer space at less than the market rate. In return, artist-tenants would be required to perform community service. This might involve giving free instruction to disadvantaged children, performing or teaching in the schools, or creating a painting for a public place. Recently sculptor Zelda Werner, whose own work has been exhibited across the United States and in Australia, spent several weeks with a high school art class to create a large three-dimensional mural for the art wing.

Criteria for tenants have evolved over the years. Initially, Phyllis saw the center primarily as an "incubator" for new artists, who would take advantage of the reduced rent and the presence of a few established artists and then move on. However, the space, rent, and synergy of Noyes are such that few artists have felt like moving on, and the EAC has been reluctant to push them out. The council, the EAC's executive director, Joseph Zendell, and the staff give strong preference to Evanston-based artists, heavily weigh proposed community service, require affirmative action efforts, and seek a mix of artists from all disciplines. Current tenants include painters, sculptors, photographers, jewelry makers, costume designers, musicians, writers, and dance and theater companies. These artists create, teach, exhibit, and perform. One of the first tenants, still present, is the Piven Theatre Workshop, many of whose young students, including Aidan Quinn and John and Joan Cusack, have gone on to successful film and stage careers.

The tenancy of the Piven Theatre Workshop and others was tenuous for the center's first several years. The building was in desperate need of a new roof and other internal and external renovation. After much debate, the City Council agreed to pay for about half of the needed repairs on one condition: the remainder of the money had to be raised through private means. Phyllis turned the pocket-picking over to residents Shel Newberger and Rich Lassar. The Noyes Renovation Fund-raising Campaign eventually raised $160,000. The city then contributed $120,000.

During a typical week in the fall of 1993, a visitor could enter the Noyes Cultural Arts Center and see an exhibition featuring self-portrait works by most of the resident artists. In his studio, artist Richard

Halstead was working on a commissioned portrait of a Chicago executive. In the halls, young girls in leotards hurried to their classes at the June Willhite Dance Studio. And onstage, the Next Theatre Company rehearsed its first play of the new season.

Phyllis, who has moved from the Arts Council to another new venture—starting a day-care program at Northwestern University—views the activity at Noyes with great pride. "I believe we were the first community in the country to find such a positive use for a shuttered school," she says. "It's a model that has been and can be followed almost anywhere."

For further information, contact
Evanston Arts Council, Noyes Cultural Arts Center,
927 Noyes St., Evanston, IL 60201.
Phone: 708-491-0266.

In the Running

DICK TRAUM AND THE ACHILLES TRACK CLUB

The program: An organization encourages people with all kinds of disabilities to participate in long-distance running— including events for the general public—by providing support, training, technical expertise, and volunteer companions.

The runner with the artificial leg thought he knew why he was slowing down. He was in a thirteen-mile race through New York City, and it was ninety-five degrees out. He had never competed at this great a distance before, or in this kind of heat. The volunteer running at his shoulder kept pouring water on him, but it didn't seem to help. His leg was feeling heavier and heavier.

The pair finally reached the finish line in Central Park. One third of those who had started the race on two good legs had quit along the way. Congratulations came raining down.

The runner began to remove his prosthesis *It still feels heavy,* he thought. He continued, and as the leg came off, he smiled. "I turned it upside down, and about a quart of water came out," says Dick Traum, laughing. "Everything that had been poured over my head had gone straight into my leg." Talk about mainstreaming!

It is the good fortune of thousands of runners from across the United States and around the world that this incident in August 1976 did not dampen Dick's enthusiasm for the sport. Three months later, he opened the door for people with disabilities who wanted to compete in athletic events for the general public by becoming the first "physically challenged" runner to compete in the New York City marathon. And in the ensuing years, he and his fellow volunteers at the Achilles Track Club (ATC) have escorted people with all types of disabilities—visual impairment, stroke, cerebral palsy, paraplegia, arthritis, epilepsy, amputation, polio, multiple sclerosis, cystic fibrosis, traumatic head injury, and others—across finish lines around the world.

The ATC began humbly in 1983 as a not-for-profit division of the famed New York Road Runners Club. There was but one chapter—in Manhattan—with about ten members. Today there are over thirty-five chapters across the United States and more than one hundred additional chapters in twenty-one countries, including China, Russia, Poland, South Africa, and Mongolia. Thanks to the beneficence of the Road Runners Club, says Dick, funds exist for continued expansion in this country and abroad.

It might be said that the ATC came into existence by accident. One day in 1965, Dick was standing next to his car at a New York City gas station when another vehicle hit him from behind. One leg was too badly damaged to save. Doctors amputated it above the knee. Dick was a twenty-five-year-old New York University graduate student at the time. After several weeks in the hospital, he was fitted with an artificial leg. He returned to school, earned his master's in industrial psychology, and went to work for the Celanese Corporation as a behavioral scientist. In 1970 he formed his own consulting company.

By 1975 the company was in good shape, but Dick wasn't. An excellent athlete who had wrestled in college, he had put on a considerable amount of weight after his accident. When a young acquaintance dropped dead of a heart attack, a mutual friend suggested that Dick begin exercising lest the same fate befall him. "I thought I had been exercising," Dick now says. "Of course, I considered it exercise to take the long walk from my office to the bathroom." In his defense, it should be noted that he also played an occasional game of tennis or softball and was one of the first amputees to ski. These infrequent athletic forays, however, were not enough to keep him fit, so he joined an exercise program at New York's WestSide YMCA.

The program included situps and pushups followed by a run. "If you didn't do the run, you weren't allowed in the class," says Dick. So Dick ran. Within a few months he was jogging for about ten to twelve minutes at a stretch. Then he jogged his first mile. "It was exciting," he says "I got caught up in it. I thought, *Okay, you can do a mile, but can you do two miles?*"

Working with WestSide's running coach, Bob Glover, he ran two miles and built his endurance up to forty-five minutes. In May 1976, he entered a five-mile YMCA race and finished in one hour and twelve minutes Three months later he completed the thirteen-mile race carrying the extra water in his leg. In November 1976, New York City marathon founder Fred Lebow invited him to run his first marathon. He did, starting four hours ahead of the pack and finishing several hours behind the winner.

Over the next six years, Dick continued to run in this and other road races Among those he inspired was Terry Fox, a young Canadian with cancer who ran across his country to raise money for cancer research

In November 1982, convinced that running was of immense physical and mental benefit to all people, Dick and Fred decided to start a running class for amputees and people in wheelchairs. About ten would-be runners signed up. Coach Glover suggested naming the nascent club after the Greek hero Achilles, who was a perfect physical specimen, invincible except for one thing—his heel.

The Achilles Track Club began slowly. Six members entered the 1983 marathon. But the number doubled the next year and again the following year. Now, more than 125 members from around the world run in the New York marathon alone. Among the runners are Peti McReynolds, an autistic twenty-three-year-old who has found happiness in training and competition; Geoff Hilton-Barber, a blind South African, Dr Don Winchester, whose cerebral palsy forces him to push backward in his wheelchair; Sister Marty Gladys, a senior citizen who has angina; and Helene Hines, who has found running an antidote to her once crippling multiple sclerosis and now finishes in the middle of the pack of able-bodied runners.

The goal of the club is not to produce marathon winners or even marathon runners. "No previous athletic experience is necessary, just a desire to improve fitness through regular training," says Patty Lee Parmelee, the ATC coach. "Some will eventually realize the impossible dream of running a twenty-six-mile marathon; others will be proud to walk a block or a mile." Again, thanks to the Road Runners, club membership is free and includes races, coaching, workouts, team T-shirts, and the team newsletter, *The Achilles Heel.*

At the New York City chapter, workouts are held every week regardless of weather and are designed for all levels of ability. Warmup and stretching exercises precede an outdoor walk or run. Speedwork is provided for the advanced. All members are accompanied by a coach or volunteer.

Who are the volunteers? "Most are just runners who want to share the pleasure of fitness and sociability," says Coach Parmelee. "The main jobs are companionship and safety. Good conversation is the greatest aid to training." Volunteers receive a sheet with advice on safety and training and a discussion of disabilities. They are not expected to run entire marathons. While some may accompany a disabled runner over an entire course, others split the duty or stand along the course to provide water and encouragement.

In recent years, the ATC has added an "institutional volunteer" to its ranks. In conjunction with the New York Eye and Ear Infirmary, the club offers eye surgery to selected blind runners, most of whom are from underdeveloped countries. The ATC also obtains a limited number of artificial legs and sports wheelchairs for its members.

The modest Dick Traum says that between running races and running his consulting firm and the club, he's often too busy to stand back and appreciate the accomplishments of the past several years. "But I will say this," he adds. "Sometimes when you work in a white-collar business like I do, it seems that all you're doing is moving papers. It's hard to see anything actually happening. That's not the case when you work with these runners. We've changed the lives of a lot of men and women."

For further information, contact
Richard Traum, Achilles Track Club,
9 East 89th Street, New York, NY 10128.
Phone: 212-354-0300.

Love to Spare

FRANK AND ANNE ALLYN AND THE HEMET HONEY BEARS

The program: Volunteers coordinate a weekly bowling league for developmentally disabled adults.

Those readers who are not interested in starting a running program for people with disabilities might consider a different sport. In Hemet, California, there exists a program that could easily be replicated in any community. For the past twenty years, Frank and Anne Allyn have coordinated a weekly bowling league for more than sixty adults with emotional and developmental disabilities such as autism, cerebral palsy, epilepsy, and mental retardation. "Our first priority is to develop social skills and good citizenship," says eighty-year-old Frank, a former personnel director for the Seattle post office. Other goals include providing a physical regime that develops balance and hand-eye coordination, demonstrating the skills of people who are developmentally disabled, and helping participants to become better bowlers and experience the self-confidence that comes from achievement.

As the parents of a son with a disability, Frank and Anne have long been aware of the lack of recreational opportunities for the mentally and physically challenged. Shortly after moving to Hemet in 1972, the couple volunteered to coordinate a casual bowling group comprising a handful of developmentally disabled clients of the Valley Resource Center. The Allyns enjoyed their time with the bowlers and began actively to recruit more participants from the center and the community at large. As more bowlers became involved, Frank and Anne formalized the program, scheduling weekly sessions and keeping records in accordance with the rules of the American Bowling Congress.

For a time the program operated as an arm of the center and received financial support from a social service agency. When funding evaporated, the group became an independent association calling themselves the Honey Bears. Now bowlers pay a token registration fee, pay for their bowling, and, according to their financial means and physical abilities, help at fund-raising events.

Much of the community also provides support, both personal and financial. Parents and guardians volunteer their time on league day and at special events like the annual Christmas party and year-end banquet Additional help at the bowling alley is provided by a corps from the local chapter of the Retired Seniors Volunteer Program.

The Honey Bears receive no state or federal monies. Ramona Lanes, the site of the league, offers reduced bowling fees and free shoe rental and donates hundreds of tickets for free bowling games as rewards. The local Lions Club and several banks and businesses provide financial services, and local pizza parlors and yogurt stores give weekly prizes to bowlers. The Allyns also assume some out-of-pocket expenses without complaint.

Frank strongly believes in reinforcing the Honey Bears with rewards. Free game tickets are earned for consecutive strikes or converting splits. High scorers and outstanding performers each week receive the yogurt and pizza prizes. A bowler who scores fifty pins over his or her average receives a patch. Trophies, collected and refurbished by Frank and others, are awarded each month, and annual plaques are awarded for perfect attendance, most improved bowlers, and good citizenship.

The rewards to the Allyns are less material but more satisfying. "I've been retired twenty-five years and I feel just as young as the day I stopped work. This keeps me physically and mentally alert," says Frank, who is called Papa Bear by the bowlers. "There is nothing greater than getting a hug from one of the kids or seeing someone respond to the program."

He tells the story of a severely disabled young woman named Amy. "She was so shy that she wouldn't talk to or look at anyone. When someone addressed her, she would turn away. She didn't want to bowl. It took me several months of just sitting with her to get through to her.

But now she's out of her shell. She's part of the gang and she's a good bowler. She qualified for the Association for Retarded Citizens' state tournament. How can I describe the satisfaction from something like that?"

For further information, contact
Frank R. Allyn, Hemet Honey Bears,
1455 South State St., #200, Hemet, CA 92543.

6.
KIDS IN NEED

Senior Class
LOU ANN FREAS AND GRANDPARENTS OUTREACH

The program: When school ends each day, volunteers come and get the latchkey children. They drive them to centers where more volunteers, most of them grandparents, nurture and teach them in a safe and loving environment until their parents can pick them up on the way home from work.

The inspiration came to Lou Ann Freas after a summer barbecue in Wimberly, Texas, in 1985. The hostess, a teacher, had described to Lou Ann how several of her students hung around the classroom after school and actually begged to help clean erasers, wash blackboards, and empty trashcans. The kids were motivated not by altruism but by fear and loneliness. Their parents worked and did not have the means to provide after-school child care, so the youngsters were on their own until the workday ended several hours later. They could either stay out on the streets—a dangerous proposition—or go to a frighteningly empty home where television was their only companion. The students who tried to delay the inevitable by helping with classroom cleanup were only the tip of the iceberg, said the teacher. There were thousands of "latchkey" kids in the San Antonio area alone.

"I was absolutely shocked to hear this," remembers Lou Ann, who has four children and twelve grandchildren of her own. "To be on your own at that age a few times is one thing, but for the whole school year is something else. That conversation with the teacher made an impression on me that never went away."

In 1984, Lou Ann had "given my heart to the Lord." Now, one year later, she was certain that God was asking her to help the latchkey children in her community. "But why me?" she wondered "Besides being a mother, I hadn't done anything notable in my life."

Lou Ann dreamed of a center where children in need could come after school to do homework, play games, and be loved. The center would be staffed by a special group of people—senior citizens and grandparents like herself. "There are more seniors than ever before," Lou Ann explains. "Many have grandchildren who live far away, so they have a lot of love to give but no kids to give it to. They also have both time and life experience to give to children." The seniors would gain something as well, she adds. "You stay healthier when you're active."

Unfortunately, while confident about her ability to love, Lou Ann had little faith in her competence to create the place she envisioned. "At first I fought the call to do something," she confesses. For over a year the desire to answer a higher appeal weighed heavily upon her, but she did nothing. Finally, in October 1986, she approached the associate pastor at First Presbyterian Church of San Antonio. "I told him about the burden I was carrying," she says. "I told him I didn't want him to think I was coming out of left field with some crazy idea."

On the contrary, the pastor thought her idea was wonderful. After praying together, he and Lou Ann made plans to visit local churches to garner community support. The pastor also introduced Lou Ann to Bill Rainwater, whom he described as "an extraordinary grandfather." Bill, a retired military man, was equally enthusiastic about Lou Ann's vision. Soon he, Lou Ann, and her husband, Vern, were meeting to discuss a structure for what would be called Grandparents Outreach. They enlisted an attorney friend, Charles Franz, to help them set up a not-for-profit organization that would be eligible to receive tax-deductible contributions. They also created a simple brochure describing the organization.

In the spring of 1987, a more confident Lou Ann accepted a friend's offer of free table space at a local home show that attracted hundreds of people from the area. There she passed out the brochure to passersby, whom she wooed with free popcorn. Among the takers were two people on the staff of San Antonio's Harlandale independent school district. These educators called a few days later and said the district, with its large number of latchkey children, was interested in exploring the possibilities of sending such kids to a center in the neighborhood.

Lou Ann knew she could show the school officials that she had created the proper legal structure for Grandparents Outreach. But although an organizational structure was in place, a physical structure for the organization was not. Where would the kids actually go after school?

Lou Ann had originally thought that the students could be cared for in private homes. But this presented several problems. Since Grandparents Outreach would be operating what was in effect a day-care center, the homes would have to meet city and state standards for such facilities, and they would have to be located in areas zoned for commercial use. City officials with whom Lou Ann spoke suggested that she would have no difficulty getting a license if she operated out of a church.

Lou Ann's first meeting with the school district staff went well. When she left, they gave her a map of the Harlandale district. A few days later, she and Vern, a compensation analyst, combed the neighborhood for a church that might house the center. The district encompassed some of the city's poorest neighborhoods.

"I'm not sure I'd want you working in this area," said Vern.

"Oh, no, Vern, keep on driving." Lou Ann was certain that God would send a sign.

Soon the couple came upon the Santa Fe Episcopal Church. "Stop here," said Lou Ann.

The pastor was not in, but Lou Ann returned the next morning and described her program to the Reverend Carmen Guerrara. Taken with the idea, Ms. Guerrara enthusiastically offered the church fellowship hall, a thirty-one-by-fifty-one-foot space complete with kitchen and bathroom. The church also featured an outdoor playground.

Having found a site, Lou Ann returned to the district offices, where a meeting was arranged with Yvonne Escobedo, the principal of Flanders Elementary School. Ms. Escobedo, whose school was close to the church, was also enthusiastic. She agreed to put out the word to the families at her school when Lou Ann was ready.

By the fall of 1988, three full years after the fateful barbecue, the program was almost in place. Lou Ann was working with the city of San Antonio and the Texas Department of Human Services to make sure the program and the proposed space met day-care specifications, and she was fine-tuning the curriculum. The afternoon would include homework, games, snacks, and fifteen minutes of Bible study touching on subjects such as honesty, forgiveness, love, and responsibility.

Under law, a day-care professional had to be on site along with Lou Ann and the senior volunteers she was certain she could recruit. Where would the money for this staff person come from? And where would the money come from for supplies and snacks? Not from the children. Lou Ann and the other three members of the Grandparents Outreach board of directors—Vern, Bill Rainwater, and Charles Franz—had determined that they should charge a nominal tuition. But this fee—only $1 to $3 per day, depending on the parents' financial situation—was not intended to pay for the initiative. Rather, its purpose was to win over and empower participating families, who might be suspicious of free programs or too proud to accept something for nothing.

Then Lou Ann remembered a friend who had told her of a business contact interested in becoming involved with a not-for-profit group. The friend now offered to set up a meeting and for the first time revealed the identity of this mysterious would-be "angel": Jack Waelti, the owner of several Jack-in-the-Box fast-food franchises across the state. "When I found out Jack-in-the-Box was interested, I had to pinch myself," says Lou Ann. "I was so elated." She was even more excited when Mr. Waelti endorsed the idea of seniors reaching out to kids and gave her a check for $10,000 to fund the program.

Grandparents Outreach opened its doors in January 1989. There were plenty of grandparents on hand. Recruited from local senior centers and churches, these helpers had received several hours of training from a professional who volunteered her expertise. How many children showed up that first day? Only five, but Lou Ann was far from disappointed. "The families in this neighborhood are so used to seeing things come and go that they've become very skeptical of new programs," she says. "They wait to see if something is going to be around for a while." Lou Ann worked with Principal Escobedo to attract more children. Thanks to their efforts, satisfied parents' word of mouth, and the organization's staying power, the Santa Fe Episcopal Church is now filled to its maximum capacity each day—forty children.

Lou Ann's faith that this divinely inspired program would take off has indeed been rewarded The Children's Trust Fund of Texas has awarded Grandparents Outreach a three-year renewable grant of

$35,000 to help pay for staff, supplies, and other expenses. Corporations such as Levi Strauss have also responded positively to requests for financial support.

Using a van donated by Jack Waelti, volunteer drivers now pick up students at several elementary schools each day and take them to Santa Fe and two other churches. At each church approximately forty children are nurtured by twenty loving seniors. On a recent day, Bill Rainwater could be seen doing homework with a group of youngsters at one table while Lou Ann bandaged the leg of a boy who got hurt while playing. Other grandparents—mostly grandmothers—were coloring and playing games with the children. Soon the group had snacks, provided by the San Antonio Food Bank at only ten cents per pound (groceries are also available at monthly Parents Night discussions). Fifteen minutes of Bible study rounded out the afternoon.

Lou Ann shudders when she contemplates the alternative for these children: loneliness, fear, and the temptation of drugs and gangs. There are an estimated forty thousand latchkey kids in San Antonio alone, she notes. This gentle woman who once wondered why she had been called to the task of matching loving seniors with needy children wants to help as many of them as she can, not only in her own city but across the nation. Thus, Grandparents Outreach is reaching out to those interested in starting centers in their own communities. "God birthed this program in my heart," Lou Ann says. "I can't stop now."

> For further information, contact
> Lou Ann Freas, Grandparents Outreach,
> 145 Cardinal Avenue, San Antonio, TX 78209.

Growing Up

RON LEEPER AND SAVE THE SEED

The program: African American men work individually with African American junior high school students who are at risk of dropping out of school and turning to a life of crime. The mentors serve as role models for the youngsters while helping them improve academics, behavior, and life skills. The organization also conducts a special six-month program in which selected youths learn citizenship and other skills and then go through an Afrocentric rite of passage from childhood to manhood.

Ron Leeper will never forget the day in 1990 that the groundwork was laid for Save the Seed, a unique mentoring organization based in Charlotte, North Carolina. It was a Sunday morning, and as usual Ron was presiding over a meeting of the St. Marks United Methodist Church Men's Club. Members were discussing a mundane administrative matter when Dr. Teleeze Foster rose and asked for the floor. Although he was out of order, President Leeper allowed him to speak. "You never know when you might need a doctor's services," Ron says with a smile.

Dr. Foster was not smiling. He started reading newspaper clippings from a notebook. The articles noted the disproportionate number of deaths among young African American males, the disproportionate number of African American children dropping out of school, the disproportionate number of young African American men in prison, the high number of teenage pregnancies in the African American community. After finishing his catalog, Dr. Foster sighed. "I'm distraught," he said. "I've been cutting these out for weeks. This morning I got up and looked at this notebook and said, 'I can't take it anymore I've got to do something with it.' So I'm coming to you as Christian men, saying we have to do something about our children. We have to change the direction our community is going in. We have to try to make a difference beyond just coming here and having breakfast every Sunday morning."

Ron appreciated what Dr. Foster was saying. Since moving to Charlotte some twenty years earlier, he had been trying to make a difference in the community. In the early 1970s he had started a church youth group that discussed everything from African American history to teenage promiscuity. He had gone on to become "a community activist with a big Afro and a dashiki," and had then made the transition from "agitator to city councilman." He had just retired from the council after ten years to concentrate on his new job as special projects manager with a large construction company, but his concern for the community had remained strong. "Dr. Foster was saying something I had been thinking about for a long time," he says.

Dr. Foster's concluding words put Ron on the spot. "I don't know what it is we can do, but I have a lot of faith in our president, Mr. Leeper. So I'm going to give him this notebook and ask him to find a way for us to be better Christians."

Quite a responsibility, Ron admits. But he did not shy away from it. Within a week he had set up a meeting with Dr. Foster, the pastors of four black churches in the area, and a couple of men from the community who had been working with young people in local programs. "I said we needed a collective effort, not just one church or group," Ron recalls.

The meeting generated enthusiasm and several more meetings, but no action. Ron grew tired. "Finally I said, 'Guys, we've been talking about this for two months. I know we have a high level of frustration about what we can do, but I'm going to suggest doing something even if it's wrong. We have four churches here today. Let's identify four schools and go into them and just have a presence on campus, be it in the halls, the lunchroom, or the classroom. Let's get some men in the schools to give these children good information so they can make good, intelligent decisions.' "

How did those assembled respond to this proposal? "They had a lot of questions," Ron says. "What schools? What age group? How many kids? What do we say?"

And how did Ron respond? "I said, 'Listen, we don't have a magic wand. Last week three young black males assaulted an assistant principal and threw him off a school bus. They were junior high students. Let's start there.' " He adds that the effort might just have easily started with first grade, but that he felt that junior high students were making "life-threatening decisions that many would never recover from. They'd either drop out of school, go to jail, or die and be lost. I thought we should start in the middle, because that's where there was an immediate problem."

Having answered the "what age" question, Ron took a city map and drew a circle around the four churches represented at the meeting. "We'll each take a school within this circle," he said. Again, there was no magic to this decision. Ron knew that no matter which schools they selected, "there would be an absence of African American adult males, whether teachers or janitors, and regardless of the racial composition there would be a disproportionate number of black kids at risk."

After a lengthy discussion, Ron received the group's blessing to move forward with his idea. Then, "I met with Calvin Wallace, the acting superintendent of the Charlotte public school system, who was an African American. I told him we wanted to help, but we didn't want to be policemen or disciplinarians called whenever there was a problem in the halls. We wanted to develop positive relationships, be a support factor, not the heavy."

Wallace had one question: When can you start?

Soon. Following "proper protocol," Ron immediately approached school board members and principals with the idea. The response was uniformly positive. At the same time, drawing on his community organization and city council experience, he began drafting bylaws for a formal not-for-profit entity that could accept donations. He was assisted, gratis, by the law firm of Charlotte's mayor, Richard Vinroot, which continues to provide legal assistance at no charge How did the organization get its name? At one of the meetings, a participant said that gangs and drugs were like weeds strangling the flowers in a garden. "We have to save our seed!" he exclaimed

During the 1991–92 school year, about forty African American men from the four churches met with groups of kids at four junior high schools The men generally went in pairs for a few hours, one day a week. With ten men to a school, a pair was able to attend every day. As Ron had planned, they walked the halls, ate in the lunchroom, and spoke in classrooms when invited by interested teachers. They also conducted workshops, talking about "male things like respecting women and why it wasn't wise to be a young parent."

What did the students think about all of this attention? "Most were very cautious about these strangers wearing suits," Ron says. "Most of these kids have had a lot of rejection. There's often been an uncle who's said he's going to help but never delivers. Or a mother's boyfriend who's there for a while, gets close, and then disappears forever." With this history in mind, Save the Seed carefully screened its own members, insisting that, in Ron's words, "they show they're not like everybody else the kids have encountered. We told them, 'If you quit, you're just proving that adults aren't serious.' "

In the summer after its first year in the schools, Save the Seed raised money from local businesses to take about a hundred students camping. In addition to enjoying the outdoors, the youths attended sessions on issues such as drugs and sex. The camping, like the school year, seemed to go well, but Ron and others were not satisfied with the overall program. "Although we felt we had done something, we couldn't measure it," Ron explains. "This was beginning to look like one of those government programs. We made some kids feel good, some teachers feel good. We made ourselves feel good. But what was the real impact of going to the school and dealing with groups of kids?"

Unable to answer that question, Ron insisted that Save the Seed try a different approach to make a measurable difference in the lives of individual students. As a result of this self-examination, the program now matches each of its adult male participants with a black junior high male chosen by school counselors. At the beginning of the school year, mentor and student sit down and develop a list of goals, most of them academic. "It looks like you flunked math last year. What do you want to accomplish in that class this year?" a mentor might ask. Then the pair discuss how to achieve that goal—for example, by studying more, turning in homework regularly, or avoiding outside influences like gangs. Working closely together the pair concentrates all year on achieving those goals. The mentors meet with their students in the school at least one day a week to review progress. "If we wait until the end of the year, it's too late," says Ron. School counselors also participate, and through them Save the Seed tries (with limited success) to involve parents as well.

The theory behind this attention to academics is that poor performance in school creates low self-esteem and behavioral problems and can lead a student to drop out of school or find solace in gangs or drugs. But the in-school mentoring is only one component of the revised Save the Seed. Mentors are also encouraged to spend time with their students outside the school—to take them fishing or to church or to a ballgame (the Charlotte Hornets basketball team donates tickets).

Students are also invited to participate in an ambitious six-month rite-of-passage program. Last year fifteen young men and their mentors met one evening each week for presentations on such topics as African American history, spirituality, career development, and citizenship. In the presentation on citizenship, for example, black elected officials discussed their work, as did those appointed to city commissions and those involved in civic affairs. The students then spent some weekends doing volunteer work, like converting old buildings into single-family homes.

At one career development meeting, a black attorney discussed how he had moved from circumstances similar to those of the youngsters to a successful legal career "Seeing that it could be done brought the real world a lot closer to the kids," says Ron. Those in the program also took weekend field trips to such places as Atlanta's Morehouse College.

These activities culminated in a final ceremony and what Ron calls "an induction into manhood." About five hundred family members, friends, and members of the community attended the celebration, which was held at a local church. "It was like an African ritual," says Ron. A man dressed like a village elder asked each student, clothed in African garb, what made him think he was ready to enter manhood. The students also selected two from their ranks to speak to the gathering. One of the young men explained how he had been lost—doing poorly in school, fighting with his parents—until Save the Seed came along. "There wasn't a dry eye in the house," says Ron. Now fifteen, the youngster has decided he wants to follow in the footsteps of a real estate broker who spoke at a career development night. He now works in a broker's office after school, receiving $10 an hour.

Ron notes that there have been disappointments as well as successes One young man pulled his grades up to A's and B's, but then they dropped precipitously. The boy's mother had died, and he and his seventeen-year-old sister lived alone at home (their nineteen-year-old brother was in prison for murder) After his unwed sister gave birth to a baby, the young man's home life was so difficult that school became secondary.

Mentors, who see their students about eight to ten hours a week, can only do so much, says Ron. He dreams of the day that Save the Seed will be able to open a home that troubled kids can escape to for a few days, or a few months if necessary. Such a home will cost money, as does the drill team that the organization now sponsors, the rite-of-passage program, and the organization's two-person staff. A golf outing, dinner benefits, and support from local businesses and foundations provide the $100,000 necessary to operate each year.

Save the Seed has grown to include 150 active volunteers, including Ron, who puts in thirty hours a week. "I tell all the volunteers that they have to be in this for the long haul," he says. "To some of them, that means three or four years. To me, it means the rest of my life." All mentors are African American men affiliated with churches. Ron feels that these individuals are best suited to deal with black youngsters, but he adds that those from other ethnic backgrounds can also play an important role in tutoring or counseling needy schoolchildren.

Ron hopes to plant Save the Seed in other cities and welcomes inquiries from those interested in doing so. He tells all who contemplate getting involved in their communities that they should not feel they have to change the world overnight. "Be happy with the little steps forward, because eventually those become big steps."

For further information, call
Save the Seed,
Renaissance Place, 631 North Tryon, Suite 236,
Charlotte, NC 28202.
Phone: 704-376-7283.

The Power of One

RITA HOTCHKISS AND CARING FOR KIDS

The program: A woman has created a network of fellow employees, service groups, and community members to secure everything from toys to toiletries for needy children. Most of the children have been abused and are under the care of foster families or social workers, who request certain items for the youngsters that the state does not or cannot provide.

Nicole is five years old and the only child in her family who has not been taken away because of her parents' abuse. The family is being forced to put her in preschool, where she can be monitored more closely. She needs a lightweight blanket for school. The family has no money for this.

Joyce is the mother of a seven-year-old and a two-year-old, and recently left her husband because he was physically and sexually abusing them. The *children have never had a bed to sleep in. The only furniture Joyce owns is a coffee table. If anyone has used beds or would donate money toward purchasing used beds ($30 each), the family would appreciate it. The waiting list for used beds from the Salvation Army is at least one to two years.*

Out of sight, out of mind: This old saying seems particularly appropriate when it comes to abused children. If we don't see them, we don't think of the basic needs that their parents, foster parents, or the state can't or won't satisfy. One forgotten child needs a blanket, two more need beds, and countless others need everything from toothbrushes to paintbrushes, from winter gloves to baseball gloves.

When Rita Hotchkiss, the mother of three toddlers, saw a number of abused children in the hospital, she could not keep them out of her mind. Although her infant daughter, Crystal, had a monumental health problem that itself would gain national attention, Rita knew she had to reach out to those without the loving support system that she relied on in her hour of need. So when Crystal recovered from her illness, Rita turned her attention to children who suffered not from disease but from intentional physical abuse. Since 1987, she has enlisted her fellow employees, as well as local Kiwanis, college students, and others in the Kansas City, Missouri, area, to meet the needs of hundreds of children like Nicole.

To understand how Rita came to the rescue of Kansas City's abused children, it is important to understand a bit of her own family history. After what she describes as an idyllic childhood, Rita suffered through a brief abusive first marriage before divorcing. She then married Bob Hotchkiss. When told that she could not bear children, she and Bob adopted two infants. "During the adoption process, I saw pictures of children who had been maimed as a result of abuse and neglect," Rita recalls. "They haunted me However, my adoptions came quickly, and I was busy with my own children."

Jenny and Robbie Hotchkiss were not even two years old when Rita learned that she was pregnant. Although Crystal was born prematurely, she went home from the hospital in early 1986 in apparent good health. Rita, however, experienced a rough delivery requiring three surgeries, with blood transfusions, in ten days.

Mother and daughter went home, and all was well for about a month. Then Rita discovered Crystal blue and lifeless in her crib. She revived the baby with CPR, and paramedics rushed Crystal to the hospital, where she was diagnosed with sudden infant death syndrome (SIDS), a malady in which infants stop breathing when asleep. After several seizures and the failure of all bodily functions, Crystal was declared brain-dead. Doctors told the couple she would never be able to see or move if she survived. They recommended that the parents authorize the cessation of medical treatment.

Rita and Bob sought other professional opinions and desperately prayed for guidance. Rita "asked God for a sign, so we would know what he wanted us to do." Minutes later, Rita leaned over to kiss Crystal's forehead, and the baby opened an eye. Within an hour Crystal showed dramatic improvement. Within three weeks she was home again. Despite tests that had showed massive brain damage, beyond repair, she soon tested normal for her age. Today she is a healthy elementary school student.

During the dark days that Rita attended to Crystal in the hospital, she again became aware of other suffering children. "I heard the screams of those who had been physically abused," she remembers. One child's father had broken her back, permanently crippling her; another child's mother had forced cleanser down his throat.

Rita took the memories of these screams home from the hospital, and they often visited her in the middle of the night. She wanted to do something immediately for these children, but realized the timing was wrong. She was still recuperating from her own surgeries, and Crystal required special attention. And there was her work: Rita, a top business development representative at Kansas City Power and Light (KCPL), continued going to the office each day so she wouldn't lose her critical health insurance coverage.

As soon as Crystal had recuperated, Rita took action. She began by serving on the Jackson County Child Welfare Advisory Committee. "But I didn't feel this was enough," she says. The committee wrote and published the "Educators' Handbook for Child Abuse and Neglect" and distributed it to local schools, but Rita wanted to do more. "I was becoming increasingly aware that the needs of abused children were falling through the cracks. I wanted to help them, without any red tape, administrative costs, and delays in time." But how?

The answer came to Rita shortly before Christmas 1987, when a social worker called with a special request. Five severely abused and malnourished children had been found abandoned in a deserted building. It was too late for the state to buy them Christmas presents. Could Rita help? Of course, she said She spread the word among her coworkers, and soon they had donated enough gifts to bring Christmas to the five abandoned children and six other wards of the state

The outpouring of support from the employees at Kansas City Power and Light inspired Rita. "Helping at Christmas was nice," she explains, "but I thought, what will happen the rest of the year when the state can't help kids like this? I'd seen how quickly we were able to respond and thought that we could do it year round "

And there was certainly a need After the holidays, caseworkers impressed by Rita's rapid response at Christmas began calling regularly with requests for help. For example, an abused child had broken his glasses. The state had already paid for one pair and could not pay for a second. Could Rita find a replacement? She could. A boy who had been abandoned in a Chicago airport when he was three years old was about to graduate from high school. He couldn't afford a class ring. Could Rita find someone willing to donate money to purchase this keepsake? "These weren't matters of life and death," Rita acknowledges, "but they were important to these kids, who had already had their share of disappointment."

The idea for what was eventually called Rita's Kids began to take shape. Rita's premise was simple: almost everybody wants to give something to help the less fortunate; they just don't always know how to. She would show them the need and tell them how they could help. She envisioned a no-red-tape system for meeting special needs when government agencies and families were unable to do so. Social workers, foster parents, and others caring for abused children would call her after exhausting all other possibilities. Then she would again call on the generosity of her fellow workers.

At Christmas she solicited gifts informally. Would KCPL use its resources to help? Yes, said her boss. The company agreed to publicize the needs in its in-house newsletter, the *Powerlite,* and on employee bulletin boards.

Rita's Kids was born in April 1988, and by year's end KCPL's 2,800 employees had helped meet more than 300 special requests. Still, more help was needed Rita approached the local Kiwanis Club, which invited her to speak at a luncheon. After she finished, the club's board voted to make her program the focus of its youth service efforts.

As Rita's Kids entered its second year, Rita expanded its services. Working with county caseworkers and juvenile court authorities, she designed a behavior modification program rewarding kids for "good behavior, improved grades and attendance, and minimizing other self-destructive traits." Employees and the business community donated bicycles and walkie-talkies as incentives.

After Rita left KCPL in 1990, the employees continued to help her kids. Her current employer, Missouri Public Service, has also been supportive. Rita's Kids has evolved into Missouri Public Service's Caring for Kids program.

Rita, who is always looking for ways to help needy children, has instituted spring and fall clothing drives and linked up with a school supply drive. When the flood of 1993 hit the Kansas City area, she intensified her efforts to secure these items. She has also conceived of a novel program called Project Love Bundles. When children are removed from their homes because of abuse or neglect, they leave behind all their belongings and often wait for hours to be placed in foster homes. "The foster home is strange and frightening. Infants often go without formula and diapers all night, until someone can buy these the next day, when stores open. Older children, who may not have been able to get together their personal hygiene items, often have to go to school without the benefit of toothpaste, shampoo, or deodorant." Project Love Bundles provides age-appropriate bundles to kids moved under emergency conditions. Young children receive a comb, a toothbrush and toothpaste, crayons and coloring books, and a stuffed animal to sleep with. Infants receive diapers, formula, and an infant toy. Older children receive the necessary toiletries. Some of the items in the bundles are supplied by individual donors and businesses. Others are purchased with funds raised by college students doing community good through the Coro Foundation.

One might think that Rita has an endless number of heartwarming stories about delivering these bundles and toys and clothing to her kids. She talks about a young boy named Mark, who was in a psychiatric hospital and refused to speak. His social worker thought that a battery-powered, hand-held car might make him happy. Instead, one of Rita's benefactors provided a sophisticated electronic automobile worth several hundred dollars, which Mark could actually get into and drive around the hospital For the first time since his institutionalization, Mark laughed and talked. But in fact, Rita has never met Mark, or the vast majority of children she has helped. "The social worker has a tough job," she explains. "It's much more important that he or she be the hero for delivering a gift." Rita's satisfaction comes from knowing that one child's unhappy screams will not echo through a foster home, juvenile facility, or hospital.

Rita emphasizes that children in every community in the country could benefit from programs like Caring for Kids or Project Love Bundles. She also insists that the programs are so simple they can be easily established by committed individuals or companies. Many people have the capacity to become super fund-raisers or need-solvers. "If you have the skill or talent to do something like this, isn't it a shame if you don't use it?" she asks

For further information, contact
Rita Hotchkiss, Caring for Kids,
c/o Missouri Public Service,
10700 East 350 Hwy., Kansas City, MO 64138.
Phone: 816-331-1085.

7.
WOMEN IN NEED

Homes Sweet Homes

SPARTANBURG COUNTY SAFE HOMES NETWORK

The program: Victims of domestic and child abuse are given shelter, legal assistance, and training in living skills, parenting, and the use of community resources. Initially, families volunteered their homes as safe havens. Now a two-story residence purchased with the financial support of the community provides bed space for the women and children.

Meg Barnhouse remembers one of the first women helped by the Shelter Available for Emergencies (SAFE). Shortly after a small group of volunteers in Spartanburg, South Carolina, decided to do something about the growing problem of domestic abuse, Meg found herself on the phone with "a woman who was obviously terrified. She was hiding with her two children at a friend's house because her husband had beaten her and was now out looking for her with a shotgun."

Meg, then the chaplain at Converse College, had taken the lead in creating SAFE in 1982 because "as a feminist, I felt an urgent priority to make women and children safe." She asked the woman to meet her at a nearby park, then left her desk for the rendezvous. "While we were driving back to my office, the woman thought she saw her husband. We drove until we lost him and then went back to my office on campus. Then I made a call and found her a home."

Today SAFE has a 7,800-square-foot, two-story residence with twenty-nine beds for such victims. The not-for-profit organization has a paid staff and a budget over $600,000. But during its early years, the effort had no shelter, no staff, and only $2,500, donated by a beneficent citizen, a business, and a local foundation. A small group of dedicated women shared responsibility for spreading the word about SAFE, taking phone calls from abused women and children, and then finding shelter in local homes.

Six Spartanburg County families volunteered to house the women and children when the need arose. The victims were allowed to stay for a few days while they made arrangements for alternative housing Volunteers from the local Junior League tutored school-age children in hiding. Rules forbade mothers from hitting their children and children from hitting their mothers. The abused women were not allowed to call their husbands.

This volunteer program gradually attracted widespread admiration and support. In 1985, the Spartanburg County Foundation provided $9,000 in seed money for SAFE to employ a volunteer coordinator. The following year, the local United Way contributed additional funds to support the program. And in 1987, the Church of the Advent donated SAFE's first facility, a small thirteen-bed shelter. With support from the community at large, the current residence was purchased in 1990.

In 1992 almost 5,300 victims received assistance from the organization; 498 were given shelter, and 421 were helped with filing domestic violation petitions in court. Volunteers still play an active role, particularly in escorting the victims to court when they seek protective orders. In addition to legal assistance, SAFE offers counseling in parenting and living skills. As the organization has operated in both private homes and a residential facility and provides such a wide range of services, it can serve as a model to those in other communities who wish to deal with the epidemic of domestic violence.

Now busy caring for her own young children, Meg takes great pleasure in seeing a staff of trained professionals and an ever-expanding corps of volunteers meet a need that was not even addressed in her community fifteen years ago. "It's very rewarding to know that each woman who calls SAFE has made a crucial step in breaking out of the prison of fear," she says. "Each time a woman is helped, we're chiseling away, interrupting the cycle of abuse."

For additional information, contact
SAFE, Lynn Hawkins, Executive Director,
163 Union Street, Spartanburg, SC 29302.
Phone: 803-583-9803.

Social Redress

BOTTOMLESS CLOSET

> **The program:** An organization provides a complete outfit free of charge to low-income women who are looking for work but lack suitable clothing to wear to interviews. After securing a job, clients may choose an additional professional outfit. Interview training and assistance with on-the-job problem-solving, time management, and communication skills are also offered to help prepare clients to meet the expectations of private-sector employers.

A woman dressed in a sweatsuit, complete with sweatband and tennis shoes, steps warily off the elevator on the fifth floor of a red-brick office building just north of Chicago's Loop. She enters Bottomless Closet, a loftlike boutique that attractively displays stylish, professional women's clothing. Volunteers meet and greet her and assist her in finding the right size and the right look, beginning with a suit jacket and ending with a completely accessorized outfit. While this is going on, a new volunteer asks her more experienced partner if she should suggest that the client remove her sweatband as she tries on clothes, but the other volunteer wisely shakes her head. "She'll do it when she's ready." As she adds the pieces to her new look, the client stands up straighter and holds her head a bit higher, and when she completes the look with earrings, she triumphantly whips off the sweatband. She is ready to face the corporate world.

I have nothing to wear. Most of us have mournfully uttered that phrase more than once in our lives—usually while gazing into a closetful of clothes. While it might be true that our bag does not always match our shoes and that last year's jacket doesn't look quite as stylish as we'd like, our lament is usually born of want rather than need.

When Chicago media consultant Laurel Baer heard a woman on public radio discussing her attempt to move from welfare to work, she was struck by the interviewee's dilemma—the painful reality of literally having nothing to wear. After completing a program that taught her a marketable skill, the woman was ready to enter the job market. She had even arranged interviews with potential employers. Her problem was that she had no suitable clothes to wear and only a dollar in her pocket. Laurel's first thought was *We can fix this. We can make this problem go away.*

Laurel called several women with whom she had done business and described the problem she had heard on the radio. The women shared Laurel's optimism and vision and agreed to get together to discuss solutions. And thus the groundwork was laid for Bottomless Closet, an organization that would not only help dress the thousands of job-ready women in the Chicago area but address the image problem of women who have needed welfare assistance. The typical client of Bottomless Closet often has a negative self-image which she has to overcome, but an equally destructive problem is the stereotypical image of the woman on welfare

Donna Paulino, who was one of the first women Laurel Baer phoned and is currently chairman of the board, is a management consultant. Since she comes from the business world and not from the field of not-for-profit organizations, her first response to the problem was to do a situation analysis "The first thing you do in setting up a new business is to analyze the situation by asking key questions," she explains. In this case:

- Is the service needed?
- How is it needed?
- By whom?
- What's the level of need?
- Do any resources already provide this service?
- In what form should the service be best delivered?
- What are the best hours to deliver the service?

To get that information, Donna and others talked to the Illinois Department of Public Aid, the Mayor's Office of Employment and Training, former welfare recipients, welfare recipients who were currently in the process of trying to make the move to work, and community-based organizations that provided some type of employment readiness training. "We found that there was a need, and that there were no other resources providing for that need," says Donna. "The next step was to develop a business plan."

Donna and the other founding board members developed a five-year projection based on a demand for service. This projection included detailed marketing and fund-raising strategies. The plan also identified the roles of various components of the organization, spelling out what the board of directors must do, what community groups must do, and what volunteers must do.

"Then we started," says Donna. "We incorporated and began making decisions about what we needed to accomplish before we opened our doors—how many clothes were needed, what kind of space and what kind of minimal cash flow was needed, what other goods and services were needed. From the time we started the projection to the time we opened our doors was just over a year."

An essential part of the organizational planning involved a search for funding. Administrative costs, space, clothing, shoes, and other accessories that could not be secured through donations would require start-up capital. Board members visited the Donors' Forum in Chicago, a resource center for those looking for funding sources. There they found out which corporations and foundations offered start-up money for groups such as Bottomless Closet.

Donna remembers preparing the materials for potential funding sources that first year. "I was constantly reminded to write the proposals in language appropriate for a not-for-profit organization—language that I was unfamiliar with, since I came from the business world. I remember being told that I shouldn't refer to others who might provide a similar or related service as 'the competition.' "

Presented with a well-researched, meticulously detailed proposal for an innovative program to serve this major need, the Chicago Foundation for Women provided start-up money. The funds were essential, but equally important was the instant credibility that came from being taken seriously by a serious funding organization.

During this year of planning, in addition to seeking funding from private and corporate foundations, Bottomless Closet developed an effective public relations program. Its purpose was threefold: to bring in volunteers, to announce to the city that this resource was about to open (so appropriate community-based organizations that provide employment readiness training could be identified), and to bring in donations of goods and services.

Did it work? Says Donna, "When we opened our doors in June 1991 in the donated space, we had clothes for over two thousand women. We had all our furniture and fixtures donated, and we had a complete office donated. We also had over a hundred volunteers "

Now all that was missing were women in need of the clothing. They came quickly and steadily, thanks to the community-based organizations that Bottomless Closet had informed of its services. Referral agencies contact Bottomless Closet when women who have completed job training are ready to begin interviewing. These women come in to *shop,* each selecting one free outfit and accessorizing it with the many additional items available. When a client secures work, she can return to the boutique and select a free second outfit, which will prepare her for the new job. Because of numerous requests, the organization is also holding a twice-annual suit sale at affordable prices (approximately $20 for a complete outfit) to help clients build their professional wardrobes.

In addition to clothing its clients, Bottomless Closet tries to educate the public. Donna says that when she or Executive Director Kathy Miller are asked to speak to the media about their organization, they are often expected to deliver a pep talk on welfare reform and an exhortation to get women off the welfare rolls That's not what they do. "Those are not our issues," Donna says emphatically. "Our clients have skills. We need them in the workforce. They just need a level playing field on which to compete."

The success stories of Bottomless Closet—more than eight hundred clients since the doors opened—speak for themselves, literally. A speakers' bureau was developed to offer training in public speaking for clients, who can then choose to accept invitations from community groups to discuss their move from assistance—be it welfare, support from a homeless shelter, or support from a women's shelter—and to offer their experiences to others who might benefit from Bottomless Closet.

The organization's corporate antistereotype program has also been successful. Its purpose is to send representatives from the board into the business world to diffuse many of the myths held by corporate hirers. Says Donna, "In this era of workplace diversity, we can talk about the benefits our clients can bring and help to bring about a positive acceptance of our clients."

The savvy professionals who operate Bottomless Closet knew from the beginning that handing out a navy blue suit to every woman wouldn't change lives or stereotypes. In addition to choosing the right clothes for an interview and discussing her situation, the Bottomless

Closet client gets an important information packet that includes interview checklists and strategies. This packet is the beginning of the third program offered to clients of Bottomless Closet—the mentoring program. Clients receive a list of questions to ask the interviewer, advice about appearance, and advice for making contingency plans in the event of illness or child-care difficulties. A reading list for women entering the job market and post-interview advice ("Immediately after the interview, write your thank-you letter") are also provided.

In addition to offering this material, the mentoring program offers ongoing support to clients who find work. All mentors are experienced corporate hirers. They understand the stress of the workplace. After securing employment, a client might find herself in the uncomfortable position of being asked to finish two different tasks immediately by two different supervisors, or being assigned what seems to be an impossible job, and be unable to resolve the problem. Her mentor is available by phone to offer real solutions to the dilemmas of the workplace.

How does Bottomless Closet achieve such ambitious goals and offer such complete service? The business expertise of the founders launched the organization successfully, but in order to maintain its success and continue its growth, it requires volunteers, the lifeblood of every service organization.

One of the reasons Bottomless Closet has been so effective is its unique understanding of its volunteer workforce. "I tried to volunteer on other projects before this, and I found it nearly impossible. Volunteers are often treated shabbily," says Donna. "Organizations demand that you commit to a certain time, a certain day, that you promise so many hours per week, per month. I'm a working woman and I can't always make those kinds of promises."

Since Bottomless Closet wanted volunteers who were from the professional world and would understand the problems faced by the clients, volunteers were asked how the program could fit into *their* schedules. There was a built-in understanding and respect for their professional lives. *When do we want you to work?* became *When can you work?* More volunteers will commit if they know they can be of real service, especially if the service can be scheduled around their own careers. That respect for volunteers eliminates the need for incentives like coffee mugs and T-shirts. "We offer real incentives," says Donna. "Networking. We provide training in presentations, sales, and we offer various workshops by and for our volunteers. We also listen to our volunteers. They often have ideas about how the organization can work better, and so we implement volunteer ideas."

Marketplace savvy, extensive, businesslike planning, belief in its clients, and respect for volunteers are keys to the program's success. "Evaluating your services is also key," says Donna. "After our first year, we sent an unsolicited evaluation to our funders, different from our annual report. We informed them of the number of clients we served, the number of donations, and we used anecdotes to give life to those numbers, but we kept it specific. This evaluation is important as a look-back, but even more important, it is what directs your future."

Donna advises would-be not-for-profiters to start their organization as they would a for-profit business. "All of those materials I wrote in not-for-profit language the first year, I rewrote in more corporate terms the second year, and actually increased our success with funders. Also, if you're turned down for funding, remember to ask why. You can learn a great deal from the ones who say no."

Women around the country are learning a great deal from the people at Bottomless Closet. Individuals and groups in several cities have expressed interest in starting similar programs. Kathy Miller and the board members are happy to provide counsel.

So do clothes make the woman? No more than clothes ever made the man. But the confidence and self-esteem gained by the clients at Bottomless Closet certainly can help level the playing field for newly trained, job-ready women.

For further information, contact
Kathy Miller, Bottomless Closet,
444 North Wells, Chicago, IL 60610.
Phone: 312-527-9664.

The Commitments

THE WOMEN'S MENTORING PROGRAM

The program: Mothers who want to move from welfare to work are paired with mentors who advise them on interview skills, problem-solving, and time management. In addition to giving job-related counseling, mentors stress community involvement.

The Stamford, Connecticut, based Women's Mentoring Program was created to assist mothers on welfare who have completed a state job readiness program and who have high school diplomas or have passed the G.E.D. exam. But, says cofounder and director Louise Moss, this is not a typical one-on-one program. "We like to say we mentor *whole families* here."

As a Connecticut state welfare caseworker, Louise felt that she was already attempting to act as a mentor to those on welfare through her job. When she met Paige Oristano, a literacy volunteer whose client list overlapped hers, Louise found that Paige too felt that she was mentoring her clients. These clients were women who had skills and promise but who were finding it difficult to enter or remain in the professional world. Most frustrating to Louise and Paige was seeing a client finally get off welfare and into a job and then, within a short period, quit or get fired. The pair realized that a formal mentoring program might give these women a better chance to succeed in the workplace and at home. "We needed to have access to the right community agencies, to be able to direct these women to the right places to go for the help they needed. We needed a special agency to serve these women—to assist them not only with getting and keeping a job, but with time management and creative thinking," Louise explains.

Louise and Paige recruited other women who shared their vision to act as mentors to women who were determined to improve their families' lives as well as their own. Funded in its first year by United Way, under the umbrella of Person-to-Person, an established social service agency, the Women's Mentoring Program served eleven clients with great success. No clients or mentors dropped out. By the end of the year, eight of the clients were employed full-time; one had an associate degree in business and accounting, one was in college full-time, and four more were attending college part-time; four women had received raises or promotions in their jobs; seven had moved to better housing. During its second year, the program served fifteen new women with similar results.

Such success, says Louise, is the result of commitment—commitment to the empowerment of women; commitment to helping an entire family break the cycle of welfare; commitment of time and energy to mentor training; and the commitment of mentor to client.

What does the program do? The mentors help the clients develop important work and life skills, such as managing their time well. Since many of the women grew up in families where they did not have working role models, they need to learn about staying on time and keeping to a schedule. They also learn to develop long-range goals. Although most participants agree that any job is better than no job, clients are encouraged to think about their futures, about educating themselves for careers, and about the futures of their children.

Mentors, most but not all of whom are professional working women, go through a twenty-five-hour training program and must make a commitment to their clients for one year of structured mentoring. They are also asked to remain in a continuation program to offer support when necessary beyond the first year. The program volunteers and staff regularly monitor corporate needs to make certain that the job training is up-to-date.

In addition to helping with employment and family concerns, the Women's Mentoring Program makes certain that every client registers to vote and does some kind of community service. "We don't care who they vote for," says Louise, "or where they volunteer, but we do want them to take responsibility for and take part in their own community."

Louise notes that other communities in Connecticut have replicated this program and that similar efforts could work anywhere in the country.

For further information, contact
Louise Moss, Program Director, Women's Mentoring Program, Franklin Commons, 141 Franklin Street, Stamford, CT 06902. Phone: 203-969-0203.

Trading Up

WOMANSHARE

The program: Women extend their community and improve their lives by bartering their expertise and services on an hour-for-hour basis in this unique urban cooperative skills bank.

When Diana McCourt and Julie Wilson met for a cup of coffee in an Upper West Side café five years ago, they hardly suspected that they would end up sharing much more than breakfast and conversation. Both were in transitional stages of their professional lives, and in order to move forward, both felt they needed to consider a dramatically different way of looking at the world. Diana, a carpenter and woodworker, was considering phasing out her custom carpentry business, and Jane had just sold her corporate catering business. They both longed for an alternative to the economic world they had been in and yearned for a life of involved sharing, an intimate economy that encouraged friendship. They hit on an idea that seemed perfect for them and for many of the people they knew personally and professionally. Why not trade services and expertise among each other, hour for hour, and all involved would profit from the experience?

"I had done some bartering before, and it had always been the most satisfying kind of exchange," says Diana. "When you pay money for something, it *ends* the situation. The deal is done. It's over. But with bartering, you begin a relationship, you extend your community, you exchange more than just goods and knowledge. The bonds and the ties that bartering creates are very healing, very positive."

Diana and Jane did not start Womanshare immediately. As they met for coffee over the next several months, they continued to discuss the idea of a cooperative skills bank and read all they could about small economies that encouraged friendship. Finally, in late 1991, they were ready to start. They informed friends of their new organization and those women told other friends and associates. Diana says she knew only a few of the women who joined.

The co-op worked simply. Members filled out a form listing their professional skills and life skills and a wish list of services they desired. Diana and Jane then copied and distributed these forms to all other members, and the deal-making began After completing their work, members would call Diana, who kept track of hours in a large ledger before finally switching to a computer.

Womanshare is currently seventy members strong, and more women request membership every day. In fact, Womanshare's only problem that Diana can cite so far is its rapid growth. "We decided to limit membership to seventy because if it gets too large it will defeat the purpose of community," explains Diana. "But another Womanshare is starting right now in Brooklyn. And the response has been so great that I'm sure others will start."

After paying an initial membership fee of $20 for six months, members contribute "time dues" of three service hours to the cooperative every six months Members offer their own skills and/or professional services, such as carpentry, cooking, massage therapy. Instead of being paid for their work, they receive credit, by the hour, to exchange for other services by Womanshare members. A newsletter sent to all members announces orientations for newer members and a variety of peer teaching seminars, from "How to use power tools" to "A natural approach to menopause." In fact, there are almost as many subjects of instruction as there are members—stick-shift driving, desktop publishing, tai chi, and stepparenting are only a few Services include wardrobe consulting, public speaking, and pet sitting. Although the hour-for-hour exchange doesn't work for every skill (a doctor cannot necessarily equate her hour of service with an hour's worth of house painting), it is this even exchange that Diana says makes Womanshare so special. All work is equally valued. All members are equally valued

This extended family and community sense makes the organization work Individuals, particularly women, in a city such as New York can become extremely isolated. For years, small towns and rural areas have combatted isolation through shared work such as barn raisings, quilting bees, craft clubs, and food cooperatives. Such activities have helped people obtain goods that would not be available without group involvement and cooperation. Urban areas increasingly require the same kind of community cooperation in order to improve the quality of people's lives.

An interesting feature of Womanshare is that members are not pigeonholed in their respective areas of expertise For example, a woman who is a professional baker also happens to love to drive and is an excellent city driver Another member's daughter was getting married and needed dozens of guests and relatives chauffeured around Manhattan. "So on the wedding weekend, the baker spent much of her time driving guests and coordinating arrangements—an invaluable service to the mother of the bride, and one that would not have been affordable without Womanshare," says Diana. The advantage to the baker was that members are encouraged to contribute the skills and the work that they love to do, not just what their day job has required of them.

"There are some high-powered professional women who love the idea of Womanshare but at this point in their careers don't have any extra time to give," says Diana. "So even though our seventy members range from women in their twenties to women in their seventies, it works best for women who are a bit older, fifties or so, who have more time in their lives."

Why women only?

"Nothing would be wrong with starting a Peopleshare and opening it up to men and women," says Diana. "But we saw this group as having a very special identity for women. The kind of hour-for-hour exchange we use seems to fit women well. Women constantly give their services. They drive and cook and nurture and teach and work and volunteer at schools. Womanshare gives them a chance to form a personal connection through their giving and to participate in a community at a time when their own family configuration might be changing." Diana adds, "That's another way in which we differ from some of the goods-bartering of the sixties. For us, the trading is the glue. The group needs the practical base, but our real focus is the whole person."

For further information, contact
Diana McCourt and Jane Wilson, Womanshare,
680 West End Avenue, New York, NY 10025.
(Please send a stamped self-addressed envelope.)

8.
SENIORS IN NEED

Weekend Warriors

BOBBY TRIMBLE AND CHRISTMAS IN APRIL

The program: Volunteers gather one weekend each year to perform major home repair work for people who are physically or financially unable to do so.

Bobby Trimble, who has brought Christmas in April to thousands of needy people across America, rarely knew Christmas in December as a child in the 1930s. One of seventeen children born to cotton farmers in Goree, Texas, he and his family had lost two homes to poverty by the time he was eight. "That's when I started working in the fields, drawing a man's wages," he remembers. Going to elementary school was secondary. "In the fall, we only went when it rained. We didn't start going regularly until January," he says. "By the time I finished high school, I probably had gone to school for only a total of six years." A drought kept him out of the fields during his senior year, so he drove the school bus to make money.

Despite being dirt poor, the Trimbles always had community spirit, Bobby remembers. "The only thing we could share was our sweat, and we did." When neighbors lost their farms, the Trimble family helped them load their possessions and move. When someone died, Bobby and his brothers helped dig the grave.

After a stint in the military, Bobby moved with his wife to Midland, Texas, where he found work as an oil scout and continued the tradition of giving Active in Baptist affairs, he helped build two mission churches in the 1960s. In 1971, the seeds for Christmas in April were sown when Bobby organized the men in the Sunday school class he taught to help widows with minor home repairs. This informal program began building momentum, and soon the volunteers were putting on new roofs and doing other major work for the widows. The labor on these projects was always free. Recipients who could pay for materials did so; church funds covered those without means.

Bobby admits that despite his work on mission churches and his title as head of the church building committee, he had little construction experience. Neither did his crew of four. But all one really needs to help in the community is a big heart and determination. "If I don't know how to do something, I can go watch somebody and then come back and do it," says Bobby. "Our roofs and other repairs turned out just fine."

Had it not been for Bobby's vision, this admirable program would probably have been limited only to needy members of his church. In 1973, however, he saw the opportunity to build something bigger. At that time Midland's Park Center YMCA announced it was organizing a community-wide vacant lot cleanup. Bobby, who insists he is a shy man, approached the Y leaders and suggested a different project. "I told them that what we were doing was better," he says. "Of course, they had never heard of us. We didn't advertise, and good things usually don't get much publicity."

Bobby was persuasive. That October, seventeen church and community groups recruited by a Y-sponsored program committee joined forces to repair seventeen homes in Midland. The committee had solicited the needy homeowners through the local media. Bobby had surveyed the homes to determine what kind of work and supplies were needed and to make sure the owners were indeed physically and financially unable to help themselves. Each volunteer group was then assigned to repair a particular home.

The project was so successful that the organizers decided to sponsor a second repair weekend in April. This time Bobby and his volunteers worked on twenty-two homes. After the weekend, the head of the program's publicity effort interviewed the elderly and infirm people who now had new or repaired doors, windows, toilets, floors, and roofs. One widow said, "It was just like Christmas," and the program had a name.

For the next five years, Christmas in April continued under the umbrella of the local Human Relations Council, which took phone calls, balanced the books, and solicited donations. During this time, Bobby continued to serve on the project's executive board and survey prospective houses. However, he became increasingly dismayed because many board members were willing to lend only their names, not their time or interest. Feeling strongly that people shouldn't be on boards if they aren't willing to work, he and Christmas in April split from the council amicably in 1979. In 1980, the state of Texas officially chartered Christmas in April as a not-for-profit organization. The next year the state honored the program with its Governor's Award; two years later President Reagan honored Bobby for his efforts; and in 1984 Christmas in April, along with several other volunteer groups, celebrated Christmas in February, when the Reagan inauguration committee gave it $50,000 in funds that had not been spent because of an inauguration week blizzard.

By this time the organization had begun to receive some foundation support. Bobby, a novice at seeking such funds, says, "I told my wife, Shirley, what I wanted said, and she put it in writing." Today contributions from foundations account for one third of the organization's annual budget of about $200,000. Individual contributions solicited by a letter-writing campaign and contributions from local businesses, church groups, and organizations each account for about one third of the total budget.

The vast majority of the money pays for building material. Last year, some 2,500 volunteers worked on 128 homes. They roofed thirty-one houses, put siding on eight, installed over one hundred windows, put in fifty deadbolt locks, and used almost one thousand gallons of paint. And this was just in Midland!

Christmas in April is now celebrated in several U S. cities. The organization went national after a *Reader's Digest* editor, Trevor Armbrister, visited to write a story. He was so impressed that he took the idea back to his church in Washington, D.C., and with another booster, Steve Winchell, led the effort to create Christmas in April U.S.A. Local chapters pay annual dues to the organization. In return they receive instruction on how to organize their repair weekends and access to a group insurance policy that covers the volunteers doing repairs. Bobby confesses that in the early years he was unable to afford insurance and "went on faith. Fortunately, we never had a claim." Foundation grants can also be channeled through the national organization to start new chapters.

Bobby is vice president of the national board, but his heart and hammer remain in Midland, where he continues to head the flagship chapter, do all the surveying, and work on homes. In Midland, the holiday never stops; repairs go on year round. "For several weeks we've been fixing up a home that burned down," he says. "A group of us do it on weekends and two or three nights a week after work."

In his early sixties, Bobby has no intention of slowing down. "As a kid, it's hard to understand when you hear that it's better to give than to receive. But when you're older and you do something like this, you realize that in giving, you're receiving as much as those you help. It's a blessing. There's not a single city or town that couldn't use this program. There's so much you can do with volunteers."

For further information, contact
Bobby Trimble, Christmas in April,
Box 3744, Midland, TX 79702.
Phone: 915-683-4177.

Friends Helping Friends

THE CALDWELL CARE NETWORK

The program: The organization refers town residents to social, medical, and religious services and provides volunteers to help with household chores, transportation, and local errands.

New York City Relief, profiled in Chapter 9, meets the needs of the urban homeless with the help of a computer containing the names of hundreds of social service agencies accepting referrals. Such a high-tech approach is unnecessary in Caldwell, Kansas, a town of 1,200 people sixty-five miles south of Wichita and three miles north of the Oklahoma border on Highway 81. There, Thelma Struble keeps the Caldwell Care Network's list of volunteers and services on three-by-five index cards in a small file box. When a citizen in need of help calls, Thelma in all likelihood knows his or her personality and situation. And she doesn't need a fancy computer or complicated software program to match that person with a volunteer, whom in all likelihood she also knows. Thus, a small town can meet the needs of its residents by promoting what the network calls "Voluntaryism and Community Camaraderie . . . Friends Helping Friends."

The Caldwell Care Network grew out of the death of Bud Goltry in 1990. His family asked the local United Methodist Church to decide on a living memorial, to be funded with a little more than $1,000 from the estate. Caldwell, with a primarily elderly population, has a high rate of cancer. The family's request coincided with a local movement to create a hospice program that would allow terminally ill patients to spend their final days in their own homes.

A four-person committee was created to consider starting a hospice with the bequest Members included Mrs. Mary Goltry, the Reverend John Thompson, hospital administrator Tom Potts, and Tracey Small, a registered nurse who had worked at a hospice in nearby Wellington. Eventually, this group decided that a hospice would be too limiting to help a great number of the town's residents. Three more citizens— Glenn Johnson, Dessie Scott, and Thelma—were then enlisted to join in a discussion of broader programs. The new body decided that a referral network for social, medical, spiritual, and volunteer services was most needed.

The network does not provide any direct care, such as hospice, home health, or medical care, but instead acts as a middleman between the people in need and the caregivers. It provides lists of services available to area residents and contacts these services on behalf of the client, if asked to do so. The network thus acts as a central coordinator to match the Caldwell community's needs with available services. There is no charge for the service.

When needs are not met by local agencies, sometimes because certain criteria for insurance are not met, the network provides volunteers, who do such things as maintaining lawns, running errands, providing meals, driving patients to the doctor, sitting with a patient while family members work, or making funeral arrangements after the death of a loved one.

After Thelma and her fellow Caldwell citizens decided on the network concept, they used some of the Goltry funds to establish a not-for-profit organization. "The attorney didn't charge us for his time and the bank didn't charge us any fees in opening our account or getting checks," she says. The network spread the word that it was "open for business" and solicited volunteers by word of mouth, by putting up fliers in town, through an article in the local newspaper, and through visits to churches and service organizations.

Each of the seven persons on the board has a specific responsibility. Thelma, a reading teacher in the Caldwell public school system, heads the volunteer arm. She matches callers requesting assistance with the fifty volunteers in her file box. Most of those offering to help are older individuals who work. "It may take ten or fifteen calls and a couple of hours before I find someone available," Thelma says. Sadly, attempts to recruit high school students to volunteer have failed.

Thelma typically receives three to ten calls a month. Recently, for example, an elderly man needed help moving his household goods to a new home; three volunteers participated. Another senior citizen needed transportation to and from a rehabilitation center in Wichita. On such long driving trips, the recipient will sometimes pay for gas if he or she can afford it. Another gentleman asked for someone to come to his house, help make out a grocery list, do the shopping, and come back and cook a meal. To avoid any difficulties with food, Thelma asks about allergies. She adds, "I know a lot about the cooking of our volunteers, so I can usually pair up the right people." Confidentiality is always respected.

Thelma also receives calls from people who need medical equipment. The network will lend, rent, or buy commodes, crutches, canes, or wheelchairs for those unable to afford to do so. Such equipment—some donated, some purchased—is stored at the local hospital for the organization.

There are certain things that the network will not authorize its volunteers to do, among them lifting people and dispensing medicine. Thelma also makes it clear that the handful of self-sufficient people who periodically try to take advantage of the network are not appreciated. But these people constitute a small minority of would-be recipients. More typical is the indigent person who wants to pay for services provided. "We say, 'No, we're volunteers,' " Thelma says.

For further information, contact
Thelma P. Struble, Caldwell Care Network,
111 South Osage Street, Caldwell, KS 67022-1644.

Volunteer Driven

CARE CARS FOR ELDERS

The program: Volunteers transport and accompany older adults to essential services.

Communities a bit larger than Caldwell, Kansas, may not be able to rely on a Thelma Struble and her file box to provide transportation for needy citizens. In Spokane, Washington, the not-for-profit Spokane Community Mental Health Center (CMHC) has filled Thelma's role since 1984, thanks to volunteer drivers.

After surveys of senior citizens and care providers revealed a need, CMHC contracted with the Eastern Washington Area Agency on Aging to assist those over sixty years of age who are physically or mentally unable to drive or utilize public transportation Typical of those receiving help is a woman in her eighties. She was referred to Care Cars after an unfortunate incident, says Leisa Kosanke, CMHC's community relations coordinator. The woman had taken the bus to her doctor's office, only to find out her appointment was on another day. "She went back to the bus stop to wait for the bus to go home," says Leisa. "The weather was close to zero degrees, and she stood outside for more than half an hour She was immediately transported to the emergency room. Now she relies on us."

Last year the volunteer drivers in the center's Care Cars for Elders program transported such seniors over 27,000 miles on more than 3,000 trips, mostly to the doctor, dentist, or grocery store By providing this transportation, the center helps elderly people stay in their own homes and avoid premature nursing home placement, says Leisa.

Wendy Baker, CMHC's volunteer specialist, says that those requiring a ride are asked to call forty-eight hours in advance. She then matches the elderly person with a driver, who is responsible for calling and arranging a pickup time. In the event of an emergency call for an immediate ride to the doctor, Wendy has funds that may be used to send a taxi. If funding were unlimited, taxis could be utilized regularly. But Care Cars was created with the understanding that the program could work only with volunteer drivers. At the outset, the center solicited those drivers through the media, carefully spelling out the responsibilities and requirements.

Volunteers work for four hours, one day a week. Before they are accepted by the program, they must complete training sessions in defensive driving, passenger assistance techniques, and orientation toward the impaired elderly. Training in CPR and first aid are also offered, but not required. Drivers must be over nineteen years old, have a safe driving record and auto insurance, and have a mechanically sound car equipped with seat belts. They receive no pay but are reimbursed 20.5 cents per mile for gas.

"The volunteers are warm, compassionate, and committed," says Leisa. "It's not uncommon for a volunteer to stay with an individual needing assistance for an extended period of time, when medical tests are needed or other circumstances are involved." At any given time there are thirty drivers in the volunteer pool. The service is free, although the center does accept donations from those it transports.

For further information, contact
Care Cars for Elders,
Spokane Community Mental Health Center,
South 107 Division, Spokane, WA 99202.
Phone: 509-838-4651.

9.
THE HUNGRY AND THE HOMELESS

Change for the Better

THEODORE FARO GROSS AND COMMON CENTS, NEW YORK

The program: Volunteer "harvesters" from apartment buildings, schools, and city neighborhoods go door to door collecting pennies in their building or on their block to be donated to the homeless groups of their choice.

Four-year-old Nora Gross saw the homeless man in front of her New York City apartment building. "He's cold. Let's take him home," she begged her father Theodore "Teddy" Gross, a playwright, was temporarily at a loss for words. He would deal with the issue of homelessness later, he told himself, perhaps by writing his compassionate daughter a story He realized that such a story would do nothing to help the man on the street or the thousands like him in the city. But what could one person do?

Weeks later, purely by accident, he found an answer to that question. "I had gone to pick up my daughter from a babysitter in our building," says Teddy. "The babysitter's husband was there, fishing his keys out of a dish filled with coins and penny wrappers. He looked unhappily at his wife and said, 'It's bad enough we have pennies in this thing. We're never going to use these wrappers.' I'd had the same discussion with my wife."

When Teddy awoke the next morning, he had change on his mind as well as on his nightstand. "It struck me that everybody has pennies, that there must be millions of dollars going to waste." These pennies could be collected and distributed to organizations that help the homeless, he reasoned. But by whom? "I felt impelled to do it," Teddy says. "I wanted to demonstrate that it could be done instead of just saying, 'That's a good idea.'"

Teddy wanted to involve his daughter as well. So together they went door to door in their hundred-unit apartment building, "harvesting" pennies. "People were delighted to part with their change," he recalls. Father and daughter collected $900 worth of coins, which they donated to the Coalition for the Homeless, a respected organization that provides food and housing for those in need.

With his writer's eye, Teddy saw the harvest as more than mere fund-raising. Conversations with his daughter and neighbors imbued the effort with "educational and spiritual meaning." He explains, "Most people think of pennies as a resource with little value. But by gathering them all together, we realize they do represent value." At first glance, many see homeless people as being without value, but then "something inside us leads us to see that these people are of immense value and that there is a need to invest in them."

Exhilarated by the success in his own building, Teddy now saw every other apartment building in the city as a potential field waiting to be harvested by the new "investment firm" of Common Cents, New York. Wisely, he realized he would need administrative help to organize a communal collection effort. That would cost money, but he did not want to use the funds collected for the homeless. So, he explains, "I threw on a tie and went downtown" to raise grants from corporations, foundations, and friends. Although inexperienced at raising money, he was able to pitch his penny idea with great success. Soon Common Cents was officially incorporated as a not-for-profit organization, with a salaried administrator to coordinate the penny collections and disbursements.

Who would collect the pennies? Teddy reasoned that those who appreciated the spiritual and educational value of the initiative would be the best ones to recruit. Like many of the not-for-profit entrepreneurs profiled in this book, who have found support at their places of worship, Teddy turned to his synagogue. He talked with his rabbi at West End Synagogue, who in a Yom Kippur sermon encouraged the congregation to participate in Common Cents. Thirty families agreed to go door-to-door in their apartment buildings or neighborhoods. They raised $35,000.

If those at the temple could understand the spiritual element of the effort, those in the schools could understand its educational value. As Teddy contemplated approaching the New York public school system, he received a call from then Chancellor Joseph Fernandez, who had heard of the program. Soon students at several schools were not only harvesting pennies but discussing the issue of homelessness. The participating youngsters raised another $94,000.

As word spread, the media in New York became interested in Common Cents. Several newspaper articles inspired hundreds of would-be volunteers from all over the city to inquire about helping. During its first two and a half years, Common Cents harvested in 1,100 buildings and collected $340,000. All of the money has gone to organizations dealing with the homeless Administrative expenses continue to be paid from other funds.

The money is distributed in a way that reflects Teddy's belief that this is a communal effort. Each group collecting pennies can determine where those pennies will go. However, the Common Cents Round Table, open to all adult and child volunteers, must approve the designated recipient. When a group announces its intended recipient, a child and an adult from the Round Table research the proposed organization and then present their findings and recommendation. Carrying this concept further, with funding from the Surdna Foundation, Common Cents has begun a pilot program in a seventh-grade class in a city school where most of the students live in public housing. The students harvested in their own housing projects and then created their own mini-foundation to decide how to spend or invest the money they collected.

Mathematicians may have already calculated that $340,000 translates to thirty-four million pennies. Actually, pennies account for most, but not all, of the money collected. "We don't turn away other coins or dollar bills," Teddy says, smiling. He estimates that the organization has collected about twenty-five million pennies, weighing about 210,000 pounds, or 105 tons. Sorting and counting the change and transporting it to the bank is, Teddy confesses, a major logistical undertaking. "Fortunately, the banks and Brinks have been very cooperative."

With billions of pennies in circulation, the opportunities for pocket change to bring about community change would seem limitless. Teddy sees every schoolchild in New York City as a potential harvester, every apartment building and neighborhood as the source of a cash crop. Equally important, he sees neighbors talking with neighbors and parents talking with children about homelessness and other social issues.

Neighbors and parents in other cities have started their own Common Cents chapters. Teddy is more than willing to help. "Most Americans are on standby, not because we don't want to do something but because we don't know what to do," he says. Common Cents can change that.

For further information, contact
Teddy Gross, Common Cents,
Room 910, 500 8th Avenue, New York, NY 10018.
Phone: 212-PENNIES (212-736-6437).

Food for Thought

DORIS WOLFF AND GOD'S MEAL BARREL

The program: A woman, her husband, and other volunteers use their own funds and private donations to give needy people free grocery baskets and evening meals.

When the young man sitting in the town square told Doris Wolff that he hadn't eaten all day, she responded immediately. "I just happened to have a hoagie in my car for a friend. I gave it to this poor soul instead," she remembers. As the young man consumed the sandwich, Doris asked him where he lived. When he told her that he had a mattress behind the bank, Doris realized that hunger and homelessness no longer lived exclusively in America's big cities. It was 1985, and the epidemic had reached Hanover, Pennsylvania, a town of 15,000 in the countryside near Gettysburg.

Over the weeks that followed, Doris heard about other individuals and families in town without food or shelter. A deeply religious woman, she felt moved to do something, despite having just lost her own job as a clerical worker. A food pantry to help the hungry would be manageable, she thought. Soon the freezers and shelves in her basement became what she called God's Meal Barrel.

The program began small. When Doris or her husband, Glen, a machinist at a local plant, or someone from their church heard about a needy family, they would collect food donations or raise the money for groceries. But as the Wolffs helped more and more hungry people and more and more hungry people came looking for help, it became clear that some strategic planning was necessary.

Doris realized she could save money and therefore get more groceries by buying in bulk at ten cents a pound from a food bank in nearby Steelton. Whenever she had $150 in donations, she made a food run. She also learned that grocery stores, bakeries, and catering services were willing to give away what they considered leftover items. She persuaded the Giant supermarket and the Weis market to give her breads, doughnuts, and canned goods instead of tossing them out. As word spread, local farmers and members of the community with gardens also contributed vegetables and fruit. Doris and a handful of volunteers from the community distributed grocery baskets to those who were unemployed or had low incomes. These people were asked to make appointments so that Doris could gauge needs and plan properly.

Soon the pantry had expanded to a kitchen. On weeknights Doris opened her home to those in need of a free meal. Usually about forty people came for soup and sandwiches. At Thanksgiving, the number increased to two hundred.

The Wolffs' house was not big enough to accommodate the nightly visitors. Rather than scale back, however, the couple sold their home in 1989 and bought a more suitable building. On the ground floor is space enough to feed the hungry. Doris and Glen, now retired, live in an apartment upstairs. Doris admits that the arrangement increases their financial burden. God's Meal Barrel has been structured as a not-for-profit entity, and donations are used not only to buy food but to pay for the building's utilities. Where do these donations come from? Mostly individuals, says Doris. Some local businesses and organizations such as veterans groups also provide money or food.

Doris eventually hopes to find a space big enough for a dining hall, a social hall, a chapel, and a homeless shelter. Is there really need for a shelter in a town the size of Hanover? The Wolffs tell stories about a young family living in a car and about an older man living in a plastic bag out at the local cemetery. Someone saw him trying to heat a can of beans with a match, says Glen. Doris shakes her head. "People talk about New York. We have it right here in Hanover."

For further information, contact
Doris Wolff, God's Meal Barrel,
413 Baltimore Street, Hanover, PA 17331.
Phone: 717-637-5568.

Garden Angels

DORIS BLOCH AND LOS ANGELES REGIONAL FOODBANK'S URBAN GARDEN

The program: Thanks to a cooperative effort involving the public, private, and not-for-profit sectors, a seven-and-a-half-acre vacant lot in the inner city has been transformed into a vegetable garden. Neighborhood residents are given garden supplies, vegetable seeds, and plots of land to raise food for their tables or for sale.

When the jury for the second trial of the police officers indicted for beating Rodney King announced that it had reached a decision, Doris Bloch, executive director of the Los Angeles Regional Foodbank, held her breath. The verdict was to be read on the morning of April 18, 1993. That afternoon the food bank was to dedicate its innovative urban garden, just a few blocks from the area devastated by the rioting that had followed the first verdict a year earlier.

Doris, who had conceived the idea of transforming the vacant lot across from food bank headquarters on East 41st Street, saw the garden as a symbol of post-riot hope. It would provide residents of ravaged south central Los Angeles and adjacent neighborhoods with a means of growing some of their own food, afford participants the opportunity to learn marketable job skills and become more self-sufficient, and give residents a greater sense of pride in their community. Success, Doris hoped, would lead to the growth of other gardens in neighborhoods across the city. But all this would be jeopardized if an unsatisfactory verdict triggered a second round of riots in the neighborhood.

Of course, the verdict did not trigger disorder. The city was spared further destruction, and today scores of Angelenos of different ethnic groups can be found tending their corn, tomatoes, melons, and numerous other vegetables and fruits in the 160-plot urban garden. Some of what they harvest will be sold at market, but most will be taken home to feed their families. In a county where 15 percent of the population falls below the poverty line and one in four children is hungry, the importance of putting additional food on the table cannot be underestimated.

That Doris masterminded this urban garden and runs one of the nation's largest food banks is more than a little ironic. Her father was in the grocery business, but although she begged for the opportunity to join him after college, he rebuffed her. "He said it wasn't the right trade for a woman," Doris says from behind the desk where she oversees the distribution of more than thirty-five million tons of surplus food a year.

Forced to find alternative work, Doris became a junior executive before quitting the business world to raise her family In the late 1960s her husband left her with three young children and the need to return to the workplace to help feed them. Examining her options and personal priorities, Doris made what she considers one of the pivotal decisions of her life. "I concluded I was never going to make a lot of money," she explains, "so I decided that I should find work where I could do some good and help other people." After a series of jobs in the public and not-for-profit sectors, she joined the food bank in 1983. "Given my background, it was the perfect job for me," she says. "I can remember my father coming home from work and saying that stores were throwing out food that could be used to help those starving in Europe " Now food is needed to help the starving around the corner.

Until it initiated the urban garden, the foodbank, founded in 1973, was solely in the food distribution business. How did it come to sponsor food production? By chance, answers Doris. She explains that shortly after the 1992 riots, she was visited by Anne Venaman, of the United States Department of Agriculture (USDA), with whom the foodbank worked on several projects. "Anne was getting ready to leave when she asked if there was anything else she could do for us. I was looking out my window at a vermin-ridden piece of land that had been burned out years earlier, and the thought just hit me. I said, 'Look at that land going to waste. There are so many people in the community who come from places where they farmed. Wouldn't it be wonderful if we could turn that lot into a victory garden?' " She adds, "Victory gardens were common when I was a very, *very* little girl, during World War II, and I helped tend the small plot of vegetables in our back yard."

Ms. Venaman agreed that a garden would indeed be nice, said good-bye, and departed. Doris gave their discussion no further thought and had no intention of following up on the idea—until she received a surprise phone call the next day from a representative of Common Ground, a cooperative that helps community people start neighborhood gardens. The caller, referred by Ms. Venaman, offered free seeds and gardening advice.

Seeds and advice would be helpful, Doris realized, but before moving forward, she had to address one major matter. The food bank did not own the land across the street; Los Angeles did. City officials had allowed the food bank to park trucks on the vacant property. But would they permit the organization to "develop" the land into a communal garden?

Doris asked this question of Wendy Greuel, a contact in the mayor's office. *Yes, assuming the soil is safe* was the eventual answer. The recent riots had added to an already large roll of vacant inner-city land, and finding a positive use for such empty lots was desirable. The city would maintain ownership of the property but would allow the food bank to use it at no charge.

When soil samples revealed that the land could indeed be farmed, Doris addressed the next major issue—funding. Money would be needed for lumber to build vegetable beds, fertilizer, and garden equipment and supplies. The USDA, supportive of the urban garden concept, offered some financial support. Doris confesses that while she doesn't like to turn down money, she was reluctant to accept a significant amount of federal assistance at this stage. She did not want to jeopardize the food bank's good relationship with the USDA by losing its money on a new venture outside the organization's traditional scope. Thus, the private sector seemed a more comfortable funding source at the outset.

Restaurateurs in several cities across the country have recently become involved in combating hunger. Through a contact, Los Angeles publicist Lawrence Cohen, Doris contacted Susan Feniger and Mary Sue Milliken, the co-owners and chefs of the Border Grill and the City Restaurant They in turn wrote a passionate letter to fellow owners, and soon thirty restaurants had agreed to contribute $100 each to sponsor individual garden plots.

Having achieved support from the public and private sectors, Doris and her staff turned to their fellows in the not-for-profit field. Tree People, an urban forestry organization, donated fruit trees. The Los Angeles Conservation Corps agreed to clear the land, build sixty four-by-sixteen-foot vegetable beds, and prepare one hundred forty-five-by-fifty-five-foot family plots. The urban garden was taking shape.

One ingredient was still missing, however: the urban gardeners The target group included those residing in the south central, south, and Pico-Union neighborhoods, a largely African American and Latino population. The food bank designed leaflets in English and Spanish, which the loyal foot soldiers of the Conservation Corps distributed throughout the neighborhood. Special outreach was made to local block clubs, high schools, and community organizations.

One might think that the offer of seeds, supplies, and the fruit of the harvest would result in a land rush, but, says Doris, "The response was lukewarm " Why? "The people thought we were trying to sell them something They couldn't believe everything was free and they could keep or sell everything they grew. Some thought that land here was 'only for Americans.' I had to keep stressing that the land belonged to them for as long as the city would let us use it "

By the time of the 1993 dedication, there were still several available beds and plots. Not so today. What turned things around? Doris believes the ceremony itself persuaded skeptical neighborhood residents of the project's legitimacy. A touching speech by Yvonne Brathwaite-Burke, a county supervisor and former U.S. congresswoman who spoke of growing up in the community, moved many of the wary. Now the waiting list for land numbers over a hundred.

Urban gardeners make strange bedfellows. Doris marvels at the ethnic mix of the gardeners and the different farming methods they employ. Some, for example, insist that corn and tomatoes must be planted in separate rows so that the tomatoes can get enough sun

Others argue that the two must be planted together so that the tomato plants can wind their way up the cornstalks.

While those from different cultures may disagree on technique, all agree on the benefits of the program. Ruth Deanda, who farms a large plot with her husband and eight children, saves $50 to $60 a month in grocery bills. She also told the *New York Times,* "I think [the garden] made a difference, especially after the disturbances. It shows that people of different races can work together."

The Deandas grow corn, tomatoes, zucchini, cucumbers, and onions. Thanks to the Los Angeles weather, a wide range of fruits and vegetables can be grown year round. But urban gardens need not be limited to warm climates. A growing number of growing patches in northern cities demonstrate that gardens can flourish anywhere that residents are willing and land is available. In post-riot Los Angeles, of course, vacant land is abundant. But in reality, every urban area has vacant land that can be utilized for gardens. The key, says Doris, is persuading city officials or others who own such land to allow such use. Doris sees this as a logical extension of the food-banking concept: "We don't want stores or restaurants to waste their food. Why waste another resource that can produce food—the empty lots in our cities?"

For further information, contact
Doris Bloch, Los Angeles Regional Foodbank,
1734 East 41st Street, Los Angeles, CA 90058.
Phone: 213-234-3030, extension 148.

Sultan of Sweat

BOB McELROY AND ALPHA PROJECT

The program: Rather than providing services that enable the homeless to continue lives of poverty, this project offers the best way to achieve economic self-sufficiency—jobs. To insure that those for whom it finds employment are able to escape the environment of crime, drugs, and alcohol that often perpetuates homelessness, the program houses its clients on a ranch outside the city, away from those influences, and provides support services.

Bob McElroy says that if he had a penny for every person who told him that Alpha Project would never work, "we could have built the Taj Mahal." As it is, the men and women whom Bob rescued from the street have built Martin Blair's Kansas City Steak House, one of the largest restaurants in San Diego, and a number of other establishments. Despite the nay-sayers, this not-for-profit program has given hundreds of homeless people the opportunity to learn a trade and enter or reenter the permanent workforce Alpha Project has become a model studied and emulated in several cities, because of its creative methods of securing job contracts and because of the support system it provides its workers.

Alpha Project was born when Bob decided to abandon "my life in the fast lane" for a Christ-like existence. A former college instructor turned entrepreneur, he had become caught up in things material: "a Mercedes, a Rolex, fluff and stuff," he says. "And none of it made me happy." He had always felt that he had a purpose in life, but by the mid-1980s, as he approached his fortieth birthday, he still did not know what that purpose was

At a friend's suggestion, he began attending church. Soon he was involved in community outreach, taking food and blankets to San Diego's sizable homeless population at his own expense. After about a month, however, he realized something was wrong. "I was just enabling these people to continue their lifestyle," he says of his free handouts.

Determined to do something about homelessness, Bob felt he had to learn more about it For almost three months he lived on the streets, under bridges, in the parks, twenty-four hours a day It wasn't a terrible life "I could panhandle eighty to a hundred bucks a day, eat for free seven times a day, thanks to all the different church groups. I could get free jackets, blankets, and clothes, and turn around and sell them and then use all the money to party " That was the lifestyle of many he met.

There was just one problem. "There was no future," he explains "How many retired panhandlers have you heard of?" A huge enabling system provided almost everything except what Bob felt was most needed for a safe and secure future—"a solid job component."

Bob's first efforts to remedy the situation were political. He organized several large marches on city hall. Government's response was disheartening, albeit entertaining. After a throng of protestors appeared outside her offices, one public official asked them to write down their phone numbers and addresses and promised to get back to them. "These were *homeless* people!" says Bob, laughing.

What to do? "I asked the homeless men and women I'd met, 'If given the opportunity, will you work?' Most said they would. I said that the proof would be in the pudding.'"

At his own expense, Bob rented a tiny five-by-eight-foot space in the heart of San Diego's Gaslamp District, not one of the city's choice areas. He visited local businesses and told them he had workers available for painting, cleaning, knocking out walls, and other chores. "These were storeowners who couldn't afford twenty dollars an hour for a painter or contractor," he explains. Alpha Project's price: $6 per hour, per worker. To demonstrate his laborers' skills and good faith, Bob had them clean the streets and sidewalks for free.

Soon the neighborhood association of businesswomen was employing some of the men to escort them to their cars when they worked late. A company that operated horse-and-carriage tours of the city hired a few people from the program to clean out the stalls. Small painting and contracting jobs followed. "We did good work," Bob says. "Many of the men had been painters or construction workers at one time or another and were very skilled."

Initially, Alpha Project's labor pool totaled about thirty men and women, but as word spread among the homeless, some two hundred asked for the chance to earn money. By the end of the first year, many of them were working on the program's first big job. Restaurateur Martin Blair hired Alpha Project to demolish an old building and turn it into a restaurant. Over a six-month period, 128 homeless people worked on the project. Eighty-six of these men and women eventually found full-time work with other contractors or went into business for themselves.

Bob tells the story of Steve, a young man with a long police record who was dragged to Alpha Project by his sister, a policewoman. After a week on the job, Steve wasn't producing. Bob threatened to fire him. Steve saw the light, and today he owns his own sheetrock firm.

From the beginning, Bob realized that a job alone would not turn every individual's life around. Each evening he offered peer counseling meetings in the office. He also arranged to house as many workers as possible in the same single room occupancy hotel (at a discount) so they would be free from pressure to spend their money unwisely or to return to the life of crime, alcohol, or drugs that many had experienced. During these early years, he dreamed of a refuge outside the city, truly away from these evil influences. That dream was recently realized when the Department of Housing and Urban Development gave Alpha Project a large grant to secure a ranch about forty-five minutes outside the city. Today seventy workers live there, commuting to Alpha Project projects.

While the grant from HUD was Alpha Project's largest, it was not its first. Alpha Project has always been a not-for-profit organization able to accept such contributions. During the early years, as the sole staff member, Bob wrote the grant proposals himself. "I always included a cover letter explaining that I wasn't an expert at writing proposals, but that I hoped they'd look past that and see what we were about," he says.

The grant money was not to pay Bob. He took no salary. Indeed, he sold most of his worldly possessions to pay the office rent. "Everything except my 1983 BMW 320i," he says. "That was our first truck. We were quite a sight—me and four or five workers in the car and rakes and shovels out the sunroof." Eventually, small grants allowed for the purchase of a real truck and additional equipment. Now Bob and a small paid staff receive help writing grant proposals from a local professor and other volunteers

The increased staff, better transportation, and first-rate equipment have allowed Alpha Project to bid successfully for several large contracts, particularly in the brush-clearing and roadside cutting business. "There's a lot of money to be made doing that work," says Bob. He adds that because many Alpha Project workers are former convicts, they have experience in this area.

Shortly after establishing itself in San Diego, Alpha Project was wooed by several other California cities. In nearby El Cajon, a city councilperson promised free office space and work. Recently, that city gave Alpha Project $25,000 to purchase a shuttle bus. Worried about the impact of homelessness on the downtown area and the annual Long Beach Grand Prix, local businesses in that community also contracted with the organization. Visitors from Atlanta, New York, and Washington, D.C , have come to study the program, too.

But can an Alpha Project work without a selfless founder-director like Bob? "Absolutely," he insists. It is not necessary to give up all your possessions and devote yourself to the Lord, he says. It is important to start small and use common sense. "Go to a local business and offer to remove graffiti for twenty-five dollars, or to fix potholes or clean the street. Show them what your workers can do. Go to a bank. Tell them your people will do some work for a few hundred dollars. The banks all have discretionary funds they can use." One might add: contact Bob, who is happy to provide start-up counsel.

While there is obviously no shortage of homeless people, there is also no shortage of potential organizers and office volunteers. Bob has successfully recruited several retired people. "They ran the country and got us through wars and a depression," he says. "We baby boomers are stupid to ignore them."

These days no one is ignoring Alpha Project. Recalling that its protests long fell on deaf ears at city hall, Bob notes that now every municipal body and social service agency dealing with the homeless immediately calls Alpha Project for people to sit on its board or commission. And this time there is a phone number and address where the formerly homeless can be reached.

For further information, contact
Bob McElroy, Alpha Project for the Homeless,
154 Rea Street, El Cajon, CA 92020.
Phone: 619-234-3041.

Vehicle for Change

RICHARD AND DIXIE GALLOWAY AND NEW YORK CITY RELIEF

The program: A specially equipped bus staffed entirely by volunteers covers the city, providing food and medical attention to homeless people and, most important, referring those in need to existing resources that can help them with problems ranging from lack of housing to employment to drug addiction.

Richard and Dixie Galloway can easily relate to those of us who look at a major social problem such as homelessness and think, *It's so overwhelming. There's nothing I can do.* In the 1970s, the couple made a small fortune in a variety of entrepreneurial ventures in Oklahoma and Texas but did not find the accumulation of wealth spiritually satisfying. "By the beginning of the eighties I knew how to do two things: make money and get loaded," says Richard. Unhappy with his life, he became a Christian in 1981 and gave up drugs and alcohol. He attended church regularly and periodically helped people in need, but he was still in search of a project that would allow him to make a real difference in the lives of those who were less fortunate.

Visiting Manhattan on business in the late 1980s, the Galloways were shocked and saddened by the number of street people in obvious need of assistance Perhaps their calling was to leave Dallas with their three children and help the homeless of New York City But the problem seemed too complex for ordinary people to address. What could they do?

They had been mulling over that question for several weeks without success when a friend from a Bible school on Long Island called with the news that he had been given an old bus. The Galloways' wheels started turning Was there some way of utilizing the school bus—a mobile unit —to serve the homeless—a most mobile population? They decided to head north and find out.

Although pulling up stakes and moving across the country without a specific plan hardly seems practical, Richard insists that he is a pragmatist and attributes his success in business to that very quality. Once settled on Long Island, he and Dixie approached the problem of homelessness as they would any business challenge. They talked to experts who knew more than they did. They defined the need. They analyzed existing resources. They assessed their own capabilities. They factored in budgetary limitations. And they reached the obvious conclusion that they couldn't eliminate homelessness. But, Richard says, they also concluded that they didn't have to eliminate the problem. There were things they could do that would make a difference.

After months of study, Richard says, "We concluded that there were a lot of excellent programs that already existed to help the homeless in New York The problem was, these homeless folks weren't very good at getting themselves to those programs. Outreach was what they needed." Richard took pen to paper. "In the lefthand column I listed problems. In the righthand column I listed resources. And in the middle I put the bus."

The bus. How could a broken-down, eighteen-year-old school bus move people from the problems column to the resources side? With the help of a friend, Richard designed a mobile unit that would be the perfect vehicle for outreach, linking people in need with existing programs. They divided the bus into three sections. The front section was an office, with seats and phones and computers with a database of six hundred different local agencies or programs dealing with problems affecting the homeless. The back section was a medical unit, with a volunteer nurse and supplies and equipment for first aid and screening. And the middle section contained what Richard calls "our bait": food.

The plan was simple. Park the bus in an area with a high number of street people. Attract them with a free meal—a hearty soup, beans and rice, a roll, and a beverage. Then tell these "captive" people that the volunteers on the bus would be happy to help them with their problems, if they wished. The pitch would not be high-pressure. Anyone interested—homeless people, alcoholics, drug addicts, the unemployed —could step into the office. A referral would be made if desired and possible.

The Galloways christened their effort New York City Relief and their bus the Street Connection. It hit the pavement in 1990 and now parks at different locations throughout the city three days a week. A full-time staff of eight prepares the food each morning, rides the bus, and makes referrals. The staff, including the Galloways, is unpaid, relying on private contributions for their own sustenance. Additional volunteers—sometimes as many as twenty a day—are also present in the bus. They come from all walks of life. Many have never dealt with street people before, and by the end of the day, "they say their lives have been changed forever," Richard reports.

In 1992 New York City Relief distributed 129,000 meals and made over 4,000 referrals. But the numbers alone don't reflect the individual success stories. At age nineteen, Jose was a crack addict living under the Third Avenue Bridge and eating from garbage cans. He wandered by the bus when it was parked in Times Square and stopped for a hot chocolate. "They talked to me for an hour, and for the first time in years I felt hope," he says. "The counselor arranged for me to get into a residential drug program, and now I'm drug-free and have a new life." Gary used to spend his time on the streets near the Port Authority Terminal. When he saw the sign on the bus offering help with housing and employment, he approached. Counselors found him housing and a job as a messenger.

Remarkably, New York City Relief managed to help the Garys and Joses of the streets, feed all those people, maintain the bus, pay for gas, and cover all other expenses for only $87,000. Individuals— particularly Henry Buhl, a wealthy entrepreneur—provide most of the support Richard has begun devoting more time to fund-raising and has secured some corporate grants. The advertising industry in New York has been of great financial and technical assistance. The program has already been replicated in Tampa and could be set up in any urban area. Richard estimates that a bus can be purchased and equipped for about $75,000

The Galloways once lived in a twenty-two-room house with seven bathrooms and an elevator. They had three airplanes and eighteen cars, including a trio of Rolls-Royces. They live frugally now, without regret, applying the same business principles that allowed them to make money to making a difference. Richard is convinced that the private sector holds the key to solving society's problems. "Those who sit and think that just by paying taxes the problems are going to go away are wrong. People in the private sector get stuck. It's a mentality that somebody else has to take care of it, but then we find out the very skills we use to succeed in business are the same skills that we need to address these issues."

For further information, contact
New York City Relief,
1155 East Jersey Street, Elizabeth, NJ 07201.
Phone: 908-352-8778.

10.
IN SICKNESS AND IN HEALTH

The Right Touch

BEVERLY BARNES AND PATIENT PRIDE

> **The program:** Each day trained volunteers nurture female patients in hospitals and long-term care facilities by administering complimentary makeup and moisturizer. Among the benefits to patients receiving this caring social interaction and gentle touch are higher self-esteem and shorter recovery times.

Beverly Barnes did not walk into Phoenix's St. Luke's Medical Center in March 1986 with the idea of creating an organization that would better the lives of thousands of patients each year from coast to coast. She was merely there to visit a friend recuperating from surgery. But Beverly is, she confesses, "an impulsive person." And by the time she left the hospital that day, she had already set the wheels in motion for what is now known as Patient Pride. What triggered the impulse?

"My friend looked terrible," Beverly remembers. "She was an attractive forty-year-old health care professional with a lot of pride, a woman who always looked her best. But now she was sitting with her hair undone, her face pale, her shoulders slouched. I wanted to do something to help her."

The friend told Beverly that her doctor had suggested that she might feel better if she put on makeup, then shrugged and sighed, saying, "But I don't have any here, and even if I did I wouldn't feel like using it." Says Beverly, "That's when the light bulb went off in my head. I realized there was a great deal women could do to help other women in this situation "

Beverly, who has a degree in sociology, was familiar with health care facilities. Before "retiring" to raise three children, she had done research at a hospital A tireless volunteer over the years, she had worked at, among other, St. Luke's and an area crisis center for infants. After visiting her friend, she went directly to the office of Brenda Burke, assistant to the director of volunteer services at St. Luke's. There she immediately proposed a new program "I told her I'd like to help patients like my friend by helping them look and feel more presentable. I would use a safe group of cosmetic products and apply those products for them. I said it had nothing to do with makeup or glamour, but with pride and dignity."

Beverly's enthusiasm was so infectious that an excited Patty Flack, the hospital's director of volunteer services, sent her to the infection control unit to discuss logistics and safety. There Beverly was advised that she could proceed as long as she followed certain procedures, such as washing her hands before applying the cosmetics.

Within a few days of visiting her friend, Beverly again met with Brenda Burke, this time to discuss implementing the plan They agreed that she would begin as the sole volunteer, working one morning per week. She was assigned to the skilled nursing unit, which served those hospitalized for long stays. Recovering from cancer, strokes, and hip surgery, the women in this unit tended to be older. Many were without family. Many were also depressed. The nurses were to refer Beverly to those patients in need of her services and emotional support. "I was nervous that the nurses might see this as an interruption to their work," says Beverly, "but they were supportive from the beginning They thought this was something women really needed "

And it was Dressing in bright colors, Beverly would introduce herself and announce that she was there to pamper the patient's needs There was no charge for her services, it was a gift. "Some of the women were leery about that," Beverly remembers, laughing. "They didn't think there was anything free in America." Still, most patients welcomed her. She would talk, massage a hand, and put on moisturizer or face makeup that she had purchased with her own funds. "When I entered, they were downcast. When I left, they were smiling, more relaxed."

During her once-a-week visit, Beverly could see only eight to ten patients for about fifteen minutes each. She knew there were more women in this and other hospitals who could benefit from the program, and she knew she could find other women willing to restore patient pride. Expansion was already on her mind when she saw a full-page newspaper advertisement in May 1986 that announced the opening of a women's center at Humana Hospital Desert Valley. She quickly arranged a meeting with Eileen Wildberger, the hospital's director of nursing.

Eileen was most enthusiastic. The pair discussed a daily program that would service women throughout the hospital. Uncertain whether volunteers would commit to three or five days a week, they determined that subject to the approval of the hospital chief, Kenneth Levin, the institution would pay a nominal fee to cover the cost of the services. This would insure continuity. Beverly would recruit the staff from among friends. "There's a certain type of woman who enjoys this," she says. "She's caring, nurturing, intelligent. She doesn't necessarily have the disposition to work in a gift shop or go to meetings."

The program was a great success. Beverly and two friends visited about twenty patients each per day, five days a week. Fully half of the women in the hospital requested the service, and it was expanded to help those who were in for shorter stays.

Over the next two years, Beverly took the service to several other hospitals and nursing homes in the area, with equal success. The patients at these facilities were happy. Their doctors and nurses were happy. Beverly and her friends were happy. But not so Arizona's State Board of Cosmetology.

In early 1988, the board had invited Beverly to speak about Patient Pride. "They gave me a standing ovation when I finished," Beverly says. But when she asked for a letter endorsing the program, the board balked. Eventually the cosmetologists requested a site visit. Beverly took them on a three-hour tour of one of the nursing homes she served. "When we finished, the board members were all teary-eyed," she remembers.

Soon Beverly did receive a letter from them. But it was not an endorsement. Instead, it called upon her to cease and desist her unlicensed practice of cosmetology. "I was hysterical," she admits. But only briefly. Over the next several months, she stopped applying makeup and applied herself to persuading the Arizona state legislature to pass a special law permitting organizations like hers to operate. Eventually, with the help of lawyer Ray Heyman, Senator Dennis DeConcini, and other allies in the health care field who lobbied on her behalf, she prevailed.

When operations did resume, the makeup of the organization was a bit different. Patient Pride, Inc., was now officially a not-for-profit corporation. And it no longer paid women to visit the patients but relied solely on hospital volunteers to do so.

Neither of these changes came about because of the difficulty with the cosmetologists. Beverly's lawyer, aware that the organization was growing, felt that a formalized structure was needed. As day-to-day operations and expansion required some funds and those funds were most likely to be donated, the not-for-profit structure seemed best. "Ray Heyman donated his legal services and continues to do so to this day," Beverly adds.

The switch to hospital volunteers was the result of a chance meeting with Dorie Roepke, director of volunteer services at Scottsdale Memorial Hospitals. Beverly found herself seated next to Dorie at a luncheon and of course told her about Patient Pride. Dorie embraced the concept and was sure that hospital volunteers could indeed provide the continuity the program required.

As Patient Pride continued to grow and flourish in the late 1980s, Beverly took on an assistant, Kassy Rebensdorf, a retired nurse. The timing couldn't have been better. Beverly's husband, Dr. Robert Barnes, was diagnosed with cancer in 1989. He recovered, but Beverly spent the better part of a year attending to her special patient while Kassy attended to Patient Pride.

When Beverly finally returned to the organization, she was more committed than ever. "During the time I spent on the oncology unit, I saw many women without their hair and eyebrows. When those go, your dignity goes. It made an impression on me. When my husband recovered, I was a real Patient Pride junkie."

She dedicated herself to introducing the rest of America to the program. In 1987, the College of Nursing at Arizona State University had conducted a study of Patient Pride patients. Dr. Jacqueline Taylor and her researchers had concluded that the program increased self-esteem and decreased depression. Their research also suggested that the regular nurturing visits reduced the length of the patients' hospital stays. Armed with this study and a videotape about the program produced by a local television station, Beverly sought the money she needed to move beyond Arizona: funds for travel and for producing training manuals and other printed material about the program.

Most of the sources she targeted for financial support were companies in the health care field. Among these was Sandoz Nutrition, a Minneapolis-based subsidiary of Sandoz Pharmaceuticals, an international giant. Bill Rush, Sandoz Nutritions' senior vice president, responded to her query with a phone call and question of his own: Why should the company contribute to Patient Pride? Beverly persuaded him to send someone to see Patient Pride in action. "I couldn't have scripted it better if I had tried—which I didn't," Beverly says of the visit.

Initially, some doctors had been skeptical about the program. Unlike nurses, they thought it would interrupt patient care and saw it only as a frill. Soon, however, it was impossible to ignore the benefits of the program. Rita Colley, the nursing consultant that Sandoz sent, was in a hospital room watching a Patient Pride volunteer when such a doctor entered. "This is important. I'll be back," he said.

In 1990 Sandoz Nutrition agreed to fund a pilot program in the Cleveland area, and the company, along with Sandoz Pharmaceutical, has continued to provide support as Patient Pride has expanded to several states. New chapters servicing hospitals and long-term health care facilities have opened across the country in affiliation with such respected facilities as the Rehabilitation Institute of Chicago and the Cleveland Clinic Foundation. These affiliates providing Patient Pride services receive on-site training from the home office in Phoenix and follow certain guidelines established by Beverly and her colleagues over the years. Beverly maintains personal contact with each affiliate and publishes a newsletter for them. The affiliates pay a monthly fee to cover expenses.

Patient Pride volunteers have nurtured more than one hundred thousand women since that day Beverly visited her friend in the hospital. What about men? Patient Pride has served them in much smaller numbers, with varying results, says Beverly. Why? In the first place, more older men than women have surviving spouses willing to pamper them. Often these spouses are suspicious of other women who volunteer to come in and touch their husbands. Also, many men are too macho or simply uncomfortable about being nurtured in this way.

While efforts are continuing to adapt the program for male patients, the volunteers of Patient Pride are quite busy touching the lives of thousands of women. Beverly still remembers one of her first patients, a frail elderly woman named Lucille who was recuperating from hip surgery. Slouched in her wheelchair, eyes down, she seemed very sad. "I knelt and put my hand on her arm—made contact—and asked if I could put something on her lips, they seemed so dry," Beverly recalls. "She began to relax. After I moisturized her lips, I asked if she wanted some color on her face. As I put that on, she began to tell me about herself. Her family lived out of town. They'd come for the surgery, but then they'd left. She was lonely and depressed. She told me that she had been a ballerina in New York City when she was younger I kept putting on the makeup as we talked, and she began changing. She sat up straight. She was thinking of herself as a ballerina, and so was I. I handed her a mirror, and then she asked for her wig. I helped her put it on and she smiled. She was comforted. And I knew I had given back her dignity."

For further information about Patient Pride, contact Beverly Barnes at Patient Pride, Inc., 2720 East Thomas Road, Building A, #207, Phoenix, AZ 85016. Phone: 602-224-9960.

Speaking Out

NOVELLA DUDLEY AND WOMEN RESOURCING WOMEN

The program: Through workshops, resource guides, and counseling, the organization provides HIV-positive women with the information and strength they need to get medical, psychological, legal, spiritual, and financial support.

Novella Dudley first learned that she is HIV-positive in 1986. She might have learned back in 1984, but for two years doctors in Chicago attributed her ill health to a variety of other causes. This failure to associate her symptoms with the AIDS virus was symptomatic of the times. "Back then, AIDS was thought of almost exclusively as a gay man's disease," she says. "I didn't see myself at risk, and neither did the doctors."

Leaving women out of the AIDS equation had tremendous implications, Novella realized as she tried to cope with the diagnosis. Because women weren't considered to be at risk, they were largely ignored by those preaching prevention. Moreover, she learned, there existed few resources for women like herself, who were beyond the prevention stage. This realization eventually led to her transformation from patient to activist to founder of an organization that addresses the special needs of women with the virus.

When Novella came out of the hospital following her diagnosis, she wasn't thinking about starting a resource organization for women with the disease; she was thinking about surviving. "I realized that if I didn't do something, I would die," she says. "I needed to learn as much about the disease as possible."

In 1987, the gay community was the best place in Chicago to find such information. This presented a problem for Novella. "The literature was geared to homosexual males. As a heterosexual woman, I had to take the material and turn it around."

Novella quickly saw that a lack of gender-appropriate literature was only one of the hurdles facing women with the AIDS virus. Equally frustrating and life-threatening was the complete absence of clinics, support groups, and referral networks like those burgeoning in the gay men's community. The health care system was ignoring infected women, as it often does, says Novella. Sadly, these women, feeling particularly stigmatized by the illness, were afraid to speak out and demand the services they deserved. The stigma was so powerful, particularly in the African American community in which she lived, that Novella could at first find only one other woman who would acknowledge that she had the virus. "I wanted desperately to talk with other women who were HIV-positive, but they were living in silence," Novella says.

Novella, who when diagnosed was working as a transcribing secretary for a group of physicians, understood the dangers of acquiescence and the power of protest. Years earlier she had attracted media attention by organizing a march protesting conditions in the public housing project where she and her son lived. Now she debated whether to break her own silence and speak out for HIV-positive women. The death of two more women from AIDS convinced her to act. With the help of Dr. Mardge Cohen from Cook County Hospital, Novella found a forum. She spoke about her condition and the needs of women to more than five hundred people at a rally deploring the treatment of HIV-positive patients by some members of the hospital nursing staff and other employees. She then began volunteering on the AIDS ward at the hospital.

Responding to the urging of Novella and others, the hospital eventually initiated a women's and children's HIV program that included a support group. Novella admits that she initially avoided this group: "I didn't want to be around a lot of women talking about dying. But then I went and found out that most of the talk was about living." Sold on the support group idea, she applied for and got a job as coordinator of support services for a newly formed agency, the Chicago Women's AIDS Project.

By 1989, Novella was Chicago's most visible HIV-positive woman and women's advocate. While she lamented the continuing second-class treatment of HIV-positive women by service providers—particularly the treatment of poor and African American women—she was heartened by some developments. The National Institutes of Health appointed her to an AIDS advisory panel, and in December 1990 the First International Women and AIDS Conference was held in Washington, D.C. There Novella met Janice Jirau, who had cared for her dying husband while she herself was ill with the AIDS virus. Only after her husband's death had Janice learned that existing home health care services could have eased her burden and increased her own well-being; no one had told her.

Novella recalls that she and Janice agreed that ten years into the epidemic, "women of color and poor women were not accessing the services and were dying faster than men because they were not empowered and didn't know services existed." What could these two new friends do? They discussed plans for an organization that could help infected women increase their knowledge and modify attitudes and behavior to improve their overall physical and mental well-being. A manual covering all aspects of the disease would increase knowledge, they reasoned, and workshops providing self-analysis, self-empowerment, and advocacy skills would lead to beneficial behavioral changes.

Producing such a manual and designing and presenting such workshops would cost money. The pair identified Burroughs Wellcome, a manufacturer of the drug AZT, as a logical funding source. "Neither Janice nor I knew how to do a grant proposal, but we wrote from our hearts," Novella says. "And it worked." In January 1992, Women Resourcing Women incorporated as a not-for-profit organization and began its mission of empowerment.

The two women spent much of the first year reading everything on AIDS and selecting and editing material for the manual, which at three hundred pages is considerably longer than a novella. Designed for women and their families, mates, and care partners, the free manual covers everything from the progression of AIDS to nutrition to legal issues to resource information. Need a dentist who welcomes those who are HIV-positive? The manual has such a list. Novella constantly updates the material and regularly sends out additional pages to those on the WRW mailing list. The printed word comes alive in the organization's two-day "Bonding the Links in the Chain" workshop, which includes sections on the law, stigmatization, and initiating a buddy system. WRW is also planning a videotape for HIV-positive women and care providers.

Novella is a firm believer in outreach. In addition to updating the manual and conducting the workshops, she speaks to community organizations and schools and coordinates women's support groups with another Chicago organization, the Kupona Network. She also meets and talks individually with infected women. Recently she visited a woman who was actually in labor when her doctor told her that she had the virus.

Such stories strengthen Novella's resolve to fight for infected women. With WRW flourishing in Chicago, she hopes to start chapters in cities across the country. "The need exists everywhere there are women," she says.

For further information, contact
Novella Dudley, Women Resourcing Women, Inc.,
12734 South Morgan St., Chicago, IL 60643-6612.
Phone: 312-928-8031.

All's Fair

DR. GUILLERMO VICUÑA AND SU SALUD

> **The program:** An all-volunteer health and education fair offers
> a yearly checkup for the poor. Volunteers from the medical
> profession, community organizations, hospitals, and universi-
> ties offer free screening, testing, and consultations as well as
> disease prevention education for jobless, homeless, and unin-
> sured working citizens.

Dr. Guillermo Vicuña shakes his head, "You want to see Somalia? Come with me to South Stockton. I'll show you Somalia in the United States."

The forty-three-year-old dentist knows what he's talking about. Since 1975, when he first laid eyes on those toiling in the fields a little more than an hour's ride from San Francisco, he has worked to bring proper medical care to the forgotten people of the migrant camps and shelters. The fruits of his labor can be seen every July at the San Joaquin Fairgrounds in Stockton, at Su Salud, the largest all-volunteer health and education fair in the United States.

How large? In 1987, at the first Su Salud (which means "your health"), Guillermo and seven other volunteers saw about eighty people. This year, more than three thousand volunteers tested, screened, counseled, and referred more than twenty thousand people at no charge.

For most of those served, the fair marks their only contact with a doctor or dentist. Guillermo, who conceived of and heads the mammoth undertaking without remuneration, catalogs just some of the results: "We found forty-six cases of tuberculosis and twelve breast cancers.

Over one hundred people had blood pressure so high that they literally broke the testing machines." Patients were also examined for and found to have problems with immunization, cholesterol, nutrition, substance abuse, sickle-cell anemia, hearing, glaucoma, dental disease, diabetes, anemia, and cataracts. Su Salud doctors and nurses referred those in need to the county hospital, which had agreed to treat them free of charge.

Most could not pay anyway, as they fall below the poverty line and have no insurance, Medicare, Medicaid, or public assistance, says Guillermo. "These are mostly working families from the fields. They receive minimum wage and get no benefits. When they do get sick, their employers have no further use for them. These good people bring food to our tables, but no one seems to care about them. Those with power don't have to concern themselves with them because they don't vote. We have to open our eyes."

Guillermo's eyes were opened quite by accident almost twenty years ago. Fresh out of dental school in his native Buenos Aires, he was sent to the United States by his well-to-do dentist father for postgraduate work at San Francisco State University. "My plan was to develop a specialty and then return to Argentina, just like Caesar returned to Rome. I had everything ready back home," he says.

The conqueror's return to Buenos Aires was not supposed to include a stop in the farm country near Stockton. But one day, while chauffeuring an older professor whose poor eyesight kept him from driving, Guillermo looked out the car window and was shocked by what he saw. "I'm a city boy. I wasn't familiar with those working in the asparagus fields. It was a 110-degree day in June. Women were on their knees. And it just hit me. I asked my professor what kind of dental care these workers received. He said none. Then I went to the Dental Society, and they told me that no one wanted to work with these migrants, that no one even spoke Spanish. And it really hit me."

In fact, it hit with such force that the young man with a guaranteed future in South America called his father and said, "I'm sorry, but I'm staying here."

"But you have nothing there," the elder Dr. Vicuña responded.

He was right. "I had no family. I was still brutalizing the English language, and my dental credentials weren't valid in the United States." To become licensed to practice here, he would have to pass the California state dental exams. While he studied, he supported himself first as a dental assistant and then as a hygienist. After he passed the exam, he started a private practice in Stockton.

He also attempted to help those in the nearby labor camps. But it wasn't easy. "My Spanish was very different from that of the Mexicans," he explains. "And my skin was too light. When I visited the camps, they treated me as if I were as foreign as a gringo."

Through sheer persistence, Guillermo did gain the confidence of some migrant workers. Because limited resources prevented him from providing extensive care, he concentrated on preaching prevention. He urged those who would listen to brush and floss regularly and to stop sharing toothbrushes.

Visiting the camps, he quickly realized that the laborers and their families needed more than just dental counseling, so he enlisted an internist, Dr. Carlos Meza, and a clinical psychologist, Dr. Pablo Alvarez, to accompany him. These men, like Guillermo, had their own private practices, so they volunteered their time on weekends and evenings. "We weren't exactly sure what we were doing," Guillermo admits. "We sometimes felt like the Three Stooges."

Frustrated by their inability to gain the trust of more laborers in the camps, the trio turned to the church—not for prayer, but for an endorsement and a pulpit. "Most of the workers were very religious," Guillermo explains. "We went to their pastors and said, 'You take care of their souls. Please give us fifteen minutes at the end of your service and tell your congregation that if anyone leaves, they'll go directly to hell. Then let us talk about their bodies.'"

The pastors agreed to cooperate, albeit using their own words, and the three doctors finally had a captive audience—literally. "Some of the padres locked the church doors so no one could escape while we talked about prevention," Guillermo remembers.

After this successful "mass marketing" effort, Guillermo sought a larger pulpit. He visited television and radio stations that served the Spanish-speaking community and asked for air time to spread his message of prevention. Most accommodated him.

From 1976 to 1980, the doctors continued to spread their message through churches and TV and radio stations. Still stressing prevention, they expanded their efforts to provide care when needed. One might think such beneficence would earn the praise of fellow doctors, but, says

Guillermo, "The dental society threatened to kick me out when they found I was treating patients at no charge."

The cost of providing free services and the frustration of the "disorganized, chaotic, primitive" effort to serve the poor moved Guillermo to create a not-for-profit organization in 1980. A local attorney who supported the program did the paperwork for free. Over the next several years, Guillermo and friends continued to visit the camps and the churches. The dentist also began volunteering on Wednesday afternoons at a medical clinic associated with a dining hall that served meals to as many as eight hundred homeless men and women each day.

Guillermo might have continued along this path for the rest of his professional career, if not for a pastor who challenged him one Sunday in 1987. "Why don't you do more than just come to my church and talk about prevention?" the clergyman asked. "Why don't you do screening?" That summer Guillermo and a fellow dentist, Dr. Dario Marenco, organized their first health fair in a church parking lot. Six other doctors joined them to provide dental and eye exams and diabetes testing. The event, publicized in the churches and on the Spanish-speaking radio and television stations, attracted eighty people.

Word spread about the fair, and four hundred people attended the 1988 Su Salud. But while the number of people seeking medical attention grew exponentially, the number of doctors and other health care professionals willing to donate their time grew disappointingly slowly. Guillermo and the other volunteers tried to enlist their medical colleagues, with only limited success. Increased media coverage attracted some volunteers, but the breakthrough didn't come until 1990, when Guillermo was honored as Stocktonian of the Year for his efforts. This award generated publicity and gave Su Salud credibility.

As health care professionals gradually contributed more of their time to the fair's success, corporations began to provide everything from money to medical machinery. When a sales representative for a major medical manufacturer learned of the fair on a visit to Stockton, he persuaded his company to donate equipment to test for high blood pressure. Colgate gives thousands of toothbrushes and tubes of toothpaste each year.

As Su Salud's administrator, Guillermo is adamant that no strings be attached to any donations. Recently a beer company offered a $60,000 grant. In return, Guillermo was asked to post a banner with the company's logo. "I turned them down," he says. "How would it look for a health fair that counsels about alcohol and drug abuse to promote a beer company?"

The desire to remain noncommercial extends to personnel as well. None of the more than three thousand people who provide service receive any pay. Su Salud has only one paid staff person. She works year round, as the fair now takes eleven months to plan and organize.

Guillermo admits that the demands on his time have grown dramatically as the fair has expanded to offer more services to more people. He laments that between his practice, his work at the free clinic, and his Su Salud duties, he rarely has time for his family. This sacrifice would be more palatable, he says, if it were easier to enlist fellow health care professionals to participate. Unfortunately, it is very difficult to persuade many physicians, dentists, and others to give their time.

One health care professional who needs no persuading is his mother, a psychologist She has flown in from Buenos Aires to assist at each fair The initial shock of her son's decision to eschew serving the well-to-do of Buenos Aires for the poor of Stockton has long since dissipated. "I think everyone back home is very proud," a smiling Guillermo admits.

A community health fair can start small.
For further information, contact
Su Salud,
8102 Kelley Drive, Suite E, Stockton, CA 95209.
Phone: 209-472-2090.

11.
A TALE OF FOUR CITIES

Quality Time
ELISE EPLAN AND HANDS ON ATLANTA

> **The program:** A volunteer service organization promotes direct community service among concerned citizens. The organization allows participants, many of whom are busy young professionals, to choose among a variety of projects according to their interest and availability and to schedule their volunteer time in a convenient and flexible manner.

Those who lament that the current generation of young professionals has little interest in community service can stop wringing their hands and applaud the efforts of Hands on Atlanta and a growing number of other organizations across the country that involve those in their twenties and thirties in a variety of volunteer activities. "My generation cares," says Elise Eplan, the energetic thirtysomething founder of Hands on Atlanta. "It's true that many people are busy with their careers, but when given the opportunity to get involved, they will, particularly if they can be flexible about it."

Flexible is the operative word. Recognizing that most people who are nurturing young careers or young families find it difficult to commit significant time to volunteer activities, Elise set out to create an organization that would accommodate both their hectic schedules and the needs of service agencies dependent on volunteers. Thus, the more than two thousand citizens—not all of whom are young professionals—who have signed on with Hands on Atlanta receive a monthly calendar offering a smorgasbord of volunteer activities.

A recent calendar listed well over fifty projects sponsored by local service agencies that required volunteers. These projects were broken down by subject, like "Education and Literacy" and "Housebuilding and Renovation," and the amount of time, nature of the work, and contact person were clearly delineated. Among the opportunities: three volunteers were needed to work one or more Saturday mornings preparing gourmet meals for homebound people who were HIV-positive; ten volunteers were sought to spend a Saturday or Sunday restoring and beautifying local parks by planting flowers and trees and clearing streams; an additional ten were needed to build wheelchair ramps on a particular weekend. It should be noted that almost all activities involve teams of volunteers. The notion that young people will be most attracted to projects that can be performed with other young people is central to the organization.

Working with service agencies, coordinating the vast volunteer network, designing special Hands on Atlanta projects, and finding operational funding now requires a six-person staff, a sizable office, and computers. All this is a far cry from the organization's beginnings in the summer of 1988, when Elise returned to her native Atlanta fresh out of the Yale School of Management to begin a career in investment banking. At that point, Hands on Atlanta was merely a dream.

Raised to believe that community service was a worthy endeavor, Elise had spent three years between college and graduate school working on Capitol Hill. Then, moving on to Yale, she had worked with New Haven's homeless population. While in graduate school, she had become friendly with a group of young people involved in New York Cares, an organization that matched volunteers with opportunities. The concept struck Elise as one that would work in her hometown, which had become a magnet for young professionals. "Atlanta was the perfect place for something like this," she explains. "Young people wanted to find ways to get involved, but it wasn't that easy unless you belonged to a church or synagogue." United Way offered a traditional referral service, but it lacked the flexible hours and team concept that Elise felt were essential to bring her peers into the volunteer force.

Elise knew that setting up a nontraditional volunteer network would not be easy and that she would need her own team to design and create an organization. Her first task was to put together a small committee to brainstorm the concept. Over the next several months, while settling in at her new job, she met with old friends and others in the community whom she felt could help. By January 1989, she had assembled twelve committed individuals from diverse backgrounds. All were in their late twenties and early thirties—"our target population," says Elise.

The first meeting of what would eventually be christened Hands on Atlanta took place on Elise's living room floor. The discussion was freewheeling. "We talked about the concept of community involvement," Elise remembers. "I didn't want us to be tied to any preconceived notions. We had a skeleton model in New York Cares, but we needed to mold it to our community. I wanted the group to bond and come up with our own unique organization."

The group bonded and molded every other week for the next three months. It also identified four initial areas of interest—homelessness, children's welfare, house-building, and AIDS—and began researching service agencies with which it might form ongoing relationships. The legitimacy of an agency and the nature of the volunteer work that would be required were important. "We wanted to make sure prospective volunteers would have substantive work, that they wouldn't just be stuffing envelopes," says Elise. To insure this, Elise and her committee participated in a number of activities themselves. They spent weekends building houses, serving food at soup kitchens, and assisting in homeless shelters. Such work not only helped evaluate service opportunities, "it allowed us to gel as a group," Elise reports.

At the same time the founders were researching agencies, they were also engaged in the nuts and bolts of formalizing a structure. The group transformed itself into a board of directors and elected Elise as president. An attorney friend incorporated Hands on Atlanta as a not-for-profit corporation and helped fill out the forms so it could accept tax-deductible donations.

Up to this point, expenses had been negligible. But the founders realized they would need money to pay for stationery, printing, postage, phones, and other administrative costs. Office space would also be required, as would a part-time staff person once the operation began. One director suggested that every board member solicit his or her parents for start-up money. Done in a light-hearted fashion, this campaign generated several hundred dollars. Another funding source appeared serendipitously. Mike Levin, then the CEO of the Days Inn motel chain, heard about the effort, sent a check for $2,500, and donated office space at company headquarters. With a respectable bank account, the organization was able to hire a sharp young part-time staff person, Michelle Nunn. Michelle, who now serves as executive director, was responsible for running the office, helping raise additional money, and coordinating agencies and volunteers.

The group considered sending out a press release to gain newspaper and television coverage that would trumpet its creation. However, afraid of starting too big too quickly, it tabled that idea. Instead, each member was asked to invite ten prospective volunteers to an introductory picnic in the summer of 1989. There the guests would have the opportunity to sign up for specific activities in the four designated interest areas.

The picnic and these initial activities went well. Committed to growing slowly but surely, the organization expanded over the next year, with new volunteers recruited largely by word of mouth. Then the *Atlanta Constitution* ran an article about the effort, and as Elise had suspected from the beginning, young professionals came out of the woodwork looking to help. "We received more than 150 phone calls," she says. "Fortunately, we'd reached the position where we could manage the new demand."

Demand has continued. Hands on Atlanta has grown to meet needs in dozens of areas beyond the four initially targeted. It has established relationships with many other agencies and has even initiated several of its own projects, primarily in the student tutoring field. The cornerstone activity and chief fund-raising and recruiting vehicle is now Hands on Atlanta Day. Each fall more than four thousand volunteers—young and old, professional and nonprofessional—spend one day doing some kind of community service. On one recent day, volunteers donated 24,000 hours. Thirty houses were painted for elderly or disabled owners, 600 meals were served to homeless people, 930 pounds of topsoil were spread, one environmental mural was created, 85 trees and 128 shrubs were planted, six anthills were eliminated, and, as the organization's literature notes, "MUCH MUCH MORE!" The effort also raised $190,000, about half of the organization's budget. Corporate and foundation grants and individual contributions account for the remainder of the group's income.

While the staff makes certain the organization runs smoothly, Elise has kept her hand in. After serving as the first president, she remains on the board and serves as chairperson of a Washington, D.C., based network of similar organizations, City Cares of America. Not surprisingly, she has resigned her job in investment banking to work full-time in the not-for-profit sector. She is currently project manager for a Carnegie Corporation grant to the Atlanta Project, former president Jimmy Carter's initiative to combat poverty.

Although she has left the world of high finance, Elise refuses to sell short those in investment banking and other professions who seek power, wealth, or fame. "They still care about the disadvantaged," she says, "and given the opportunity, they will get involved to make a difference."

> Those wishing to provide or take advantage of such opportunities can contact
> Michelle Nunn, Hands on Atlanta,
> 931 Monroe Drive, Suite 208, Atlanta, GA 30308.
> Phone: 404-872-2252.
> Also City Cares of America,
> 1737 H Street NW, Washington, DC 20006.

Linking Lincoln
VENTURES IN PARTNERSHIP

The program: A school system and the local Chamber of Commerce cooperate to create working relationships between the schools and businesses or organizations. The lives of the students and the volunteers are enriched, a greater understanding between business and the schools is created, and the community at large is improved by particular student or student-business projects.

Barb Hopkins, former Nebraska Teacher of the Year, loves to play with matches. As the coordinator of Ventures in Partnership (VIP), Barb's job is to match public schools or school programs in Lincoln,

Nebraska, with corporations and organizations interested in bettering the lives of students and the community. Among the happy couples she has united are

- State Farm Insurance and Culler Junior High, which has a high minority student enrollment but few minority teachers. Minority employees from State Farm work individually with the students and sponsor career shadowing days to expose the youngsters to the business world.
- The entire school system and Burger King, which sponsors leadership seminars for selected students.
- Lincoln Benefit Life Insurance and the Morley School, which worked together to raise enough money to present the Lincoln Children's Museum with three interactive exhibits.

The program is not only for large companies. A local refuse firm with only four employees works on environmental matters with one school. A Lincoln architectural firm sponsors a public works design competition for high school students interested in drafting. And University of Nebraska athletes work with youngsters in the special education program.

VIP was inspired in part by the success of the Adopt-a-School model in other cities, but it is, as the word *partnership* implies, more like a marriage than an adoption. This is an important difference, one that elicits calls from across the country by school systems that see the program as a prototype for the future. "VIP is unique because of its emphasis on local control of management of partnership activities," says Barb. "Our teachers and community volunteers identify their focus, develop a structure for achieving mutual goals, and facilitate goal accomplishment within individual partnerships." While giving teachers a greater say in such program development may be unique now, it won't be in the coming years, Barb insists.

How does Lincoln, a city of 130,000 in America's heartland, find itself on the cutting edge? The creation of VIP is a good example. The Lincoln Chamber of Commerce Education Subcommittee, which initiated VIP in 1987 to prevent problems afflicting other urban school systems, was composed not only of businesspeople but of educators. Today the program is officially billed as a "cooperative project of the

Lincoln Public Schools, the Lincoln Education Association [the local teachers' group], and the Lincoln Chamber of Commerce."

After deciding to do something, the three partners went to work. The Chamber of Commerce found fourteen businesses willing to help in the schools. Barb, who was still teaching at the time, was named part-time program coordinator, and her salary was paid by the teachers' association. In addition to conducting a school needs assessment to suggest possible matches for the businesses, she had to design the structure of the new organization, institute policies, consider issues of liability, and create a handbook. She was and still is responsible to a board composed of school officials, teachers, businesspeople, and community leaders—further evidence of a broad-based partnership.

Through constant promotion, including a weekly radio show, VIP has grown dramatically. By the end of its first year, forty-three partnerships were in place. Now the total stands at four hundred, and Barb expects this number to double quite soon. Matchmaking is now her full-time job. She keeps in constant contact with paid teacher liaisons at all Lincoln public schools about what kinds of programs they might like. Schools and their partners are encouraged to be creative, and the options are limitless, from fitness to mentoring to rewarding academic excellence and a drug-free lifestyle with a discount card good at local businesses. Then, when a company, government agency, neighborhood association, or some other organization interested in helping calls, she suggests a match based on mutual interests and such additional factors as geography. At this point it is up to the school and the business or organization to determine whether they want to move ahead. Most do.

Is the program cost-effective? Yes, says Barb, citing figures that indicate a 200 to 400 percent return on dollars invested. (This is calculated by applying a nationally recognized dollar-per-hour figure to volunteers' time and adding it to the value of goods donated.) But it is not the bottom line that is at the bottom of VIP. Says Barb, "VIP is about sharing and caring. Lincoln has always been a community where volunteerism is a way of life. VIP opened the door to a new way of thinking about volunteerism. Together our creative VIPs are building a stronger city, a stronger community, and stronger schools by working with our most precious commodity—our youth."

For further information, contact
Barbara Hopkins, Ventures in Partnership,
Lincoln Education Association,
620 North 48th Street, Suite 209 A, Lincoln, NE 68504.
Phone: 402-466-4174.

Getting to the Root

FREE THE CHILDREN

The program: An organization attempts to free children trapped in the culture of poverty and to enable impoverished families to become self-sufficient by serving as a catalyst for comprehensive countywide planning and then advocating, coordinating, and evaluating policies and services.

Can an entire community develop a holistic approach to a social ill as widespread and complex as poverty? Shelby County, Tennessee, which includes the city of Memphis, believes it is worth trying. In 1987, Mayor William N. Morris, Jr., appointed a Culture of Poverty Think Tank to study the problem and propose solutions.

After ten months of intense study, the think tank presented its findings. It concluded that some 150,000 individuals in Memphis and the county, including 65,000 children, were "entrapped in an all-pervasive culture of poverty." It also concluded that only through a "holistic, collaborative, and services-integration approach" could the root causes of poverty be effectively addressed. The think tank issued a report, based on the work of several subcommittees and the testimony of hundreds of citizens, that included seventy recommendations to deal with what it identified as the root causes of poverty. lack of affordable, quality child care; escalating use of drugs and crime; lack of educational opportunities; lack of affordable and accessible health care; lack of affordable and decent housing.

Soon after the think tank presented its findings, Free the Children (FTC), a not-for-profit corporation, was formed to define and develop strategies and advocate program and policy changes that would help move poor residents of Shelby County to self-sufficiency. The ambitious effort is governed by a forty-member board of directors representing the public, private, and not-for-profit sectors as well as residents in affected areas. The mayor serves as chairperson.

FTC gained credibility and momentum in 1991 when it secured a $500,000 grant from the U.S. Department of Health and Human Services to demonstrate ways of creating self-employment opportunities, small businesses, and jobs for the residents of North Memphis' Hurt Village, one of four initial target areas. The organization then created a revolving loan fund to make small loans to Hurt Village residents or other eligible individuals starting their own businesses or employing Hurt Village residents. One small business owner, who received a $10,000 loan from the fund, opened a dry-cleaning store employing four people from Hurt Village.

On the crime front, FTC initiated contact with the newly appointed director of the Memphis Police Department, which resulted in increased police visibility and law enforcement in Hurt Village. The organization also obtained and made available to owners of vacant or abandoned buildings in target areas $10,000 in Federal Emergency Management Agency funds to secure the buildings.

Other initiatives have included helping to secure a grant that provided down payment and closing cost assistance to nineteen first-time home buyers, developing the concept of a city Housing Information and Resource Center, and organizing a citywide campaign to immunize preschool children. FTC even established a children's community choir, which was named the best new community choir for 1991 by the Gospel Music Hall of Fame.

FTC's holistic approach may not be gospel yet, but it has attracted a great deal of attention. Tennessean Tipper Gore was involved with the organization until her move to Washington, D.C., in 1993. Senators and cabinet members have paid visits, as have foreign dignitaries and, perhaps most important, representatives from several U.S. cities interested in emulating the model.

For further information, contact
John Baker, Director of Program Operations, Free the Children,
1192 Peabody, Memphis, TN 38104.
Phone: 901-276-0843.

Different Tacks

SENIOR CITIZEN TAX WORK-OFF PROGRAM

The program: Senior citizens work off their city property taxes by volunteering in city departments.

Suzanne Jarboe-Simpson, the volunteer program coordinator for the city of Fort Collins, Colorado, describes the Senior Citizen Tax Work-Off Program as "win-win" Senior residents benefit because they earn money specifically to pay their city property taxes. And Fort Collins gains because it receives needed work from a talented pool of residents at a reasonable price.

The citizens of Fort Collins (population about 100,000) have long been community-spirited, says Carolyn Andrews, the assistant director of the local Volunteer Clearinghouse. Since 1966, this not-for-profit organization has matched volunteers with private social service agencies. The city also operates a volunteer effort, matching willing residents of all ages with openings in government departments and programs—parks and recreation, the library, the performing arts center, and other municipal venues.

In 1980, the city added a unique twist to its volunteer initiative after members of its senior advisory board expressed concerns about the ability of the elderly to pay rising property taxes. Each winter the city publicizes the tax work-off program through local newspapers and television stations and as part of the monthly utility bill insert. Interested seniors meet with program coordinators and fill out a simple application form indicating areas of interest and the number of hours they are eligible to work as defined by the dollar amount of their property taxes. The city pays the prevailing minimum wage to those placed in tax work-off positions. These citizens can then apply the money they earn to their property taxes. Their tax work-off pay cannot exceed their city tax assessment, although they are free to work additional hours without compensation

The program is currently open to all city residents who are sixty years old and older. There is no income criterion, as other programs exist to address the needs of those with low incomes. About ninety senior citizens apply to the program each year. Larimer County, which includes Fort Collins, runs a similar program that allows senior residents to participate in a countywide tax work-off program. The city and county have joined forces to create a single application.

Suzanne says that "the program's return to the city is manifold. Senior citizens no longer fear being forced out of their homes by rising taxes. They enjoy the work, and many remain in the system long after their taxes have been paid. Each year many seniors are requested by the departments they have previously worked for, lending continuity to the program and decreasing training time."

For further information, contact
City of Fort Collins, Employee Development,
P.O. Box 580, Fort Collins, CO 80522.

PART 2:
Student and
School Initiatives

12.
IN THE SCHOOLS

Getting the Drop on Dropouts

LAMAR HIGH SCHOOL'S LITTLE VIKINGS PROGRAM

The program: High school homerooms "adopt" elementary school students identified as potential dropouts. The high school students provide friendship and academic support to encourage the youngsters to stay in school—tutoring, going on field trips, organizing activities, and donating clothing and toys at Christmas.

The letter begins with a drawing of presents under a Christmas tree. Then,

> *Dear Big Vikes:*
> *Thank you so much for my wonderful Christmas presents. I loved them all. . . . I will be wearing the clothes to school. I moved to Arlington two years ago and it's the best thing to happen to me. You were so sweet to be nice to me. I really do love you.*

Everyone loves the Little Vikings program at Lamar High School in Arlington, Texas: the seventy-plus participating elementary school students, who receive far more than Christmas gifts; the 1,700 participating Lamar students, who learn the meaning of giving and themselves experience increased self-esteem; the teachers at the participating schools, who see improved attendance and academic performance, a lower dropout rate, and happier children; and the Lamar administration, which marvels that the program is an even greater unifying force than the high school's always successful, highly popular Vikings football team.

The program has even attracted the eyes of the Texas state government, which in 1991 bestowed a $100,000 Governor's Award on the school. Assistant Principal Julie Porter confesses that Lamar was stunned as well as gratified by the award, which will endow the program for many years to come. But she is quick to note that such a program "can begin with no initial costs if your students and area businesses are willing to donate food, gifts, and clothing." Activities can be planned that require only minimal expense. Local amusement centers and businesses often offer free or reduced admissions for field trips. And academic tutoring does not require funds. "The program does not rely on money," Julie concludes. "It only requires a commitment of time and love."

Little Vikings was the brainchild not of the Lamar administration but of loving students who were willing to commit the time to make a difference in their community. In June 1988, student council officers returned from a statewide leadership conference inspired to begin a mentoring program for younger children. They approached Principal Weldon English, who arranged a meeting with several school officials.

The officers' timing could not have been better. Arlington, a city adjacent to Dallas, had grown increasingly concerned about the rise in its dropout rate, and discussions had recently begun among concerned parents, teachers, and city officials. "Many people address the dropout problem at the high school level. Our research had shown that a large number of children were dropping out before high school but that no one was focusing on these little kids," says Julie Porter. "We liked the idea that our students wanted to concentrate on this at-risk group."

The Lamar High administration identified two Arlington elementary schools with youngsters who would benefit from a mentoring program. When approached by the officers and their faculty sponsor, Jane Borland, the principals at these schools were understandably enthusiastic and quickly set up meetings to discuss program ideas. To involve everyone at the high school, the Lamar officers and administration decided that each homeroom would sponsor one or more of the approximately seventy elementary school students identified by their principals as potential dropouts—kids with a sudden drop in grades or repeated disciplinary and behavior problems; children of teenage parents; those experiencing family changes or difficulties; those from poverty-stricken homes.

A time-tested, simple activity was chosen to kick off what was named the Little Vikings program. Just before the school Christmas break, the Little Vikings arrived at the high school to meet their new friends and open packages of toys and clothing purchased or donated by the Big Vikes. Says Julie, "The morning of the party was not quite typical. There were skateboards, bicycles, and remote-controlled toys dashing through the halls, Barbie dolls waltzing through the building, and little girls in new dresses and coats. And there were nearly 1,700 teary-eyed high schoolers touched by the joy they had given to a less fortunate youngster." After the party, truckloads of food and gifts made their way to the children's families.

Lamar students now provide activities and remembrances on other holidays and special occasions for the Little Vikings and their families. They host a Halloween carnival and hot dog party, a Thanksgiving dinner, field trips to the zoo, movies, and museums, roller-skating parties, Easter egg hunts, and an end-of-the-year awards assembly. The young students also receive cards and gifts on their birthdays.

But more is needed to convey the mentoring program's message: "Stay in school and you have an alternative to a life of drugs and alcohol, unwanted pregnancies, and the emotional issues that often stand in the way of a successful and productive life." To help the Little Vikings achieve academic excellence and to encourage the children, a tutoring component complements the social activities. Before- and after-school tutoring is scheduled at each elementary school. Lamar student volunteers visit the schools at least twice a week, focusing on the Little Vikings but offering their services to the entire student body.

Julie acknowledges that orchestrating such an ambitious program, which involves all Lamar students, requires tremendous cooperation with the feeder schools and is time-consuming for the Lamar administration and student council officers. But she says, "To meet the goal of keeping kids in school, numerous activities must be planned to allow contact between the Little Vikings and the Lamar students. Much of the encouragement must come on an individualized basis." Parents, the PTA, and service clubs such as the Rotary have also contributed essential people-power and funds.

Does all of this energy and enthusiasm translate into a successful program? Yes, say the elementary school principals. They note that the Little Vikings have become more enthusiastic about school and attend more regularly. Many have shown marked improvement in grades. Some have become more outgoing and confident. Attendance in the tutoring program grew from ten to fifteen students per day to fifty to seventy in just three years.

While the Little Vikings program was devised to benefit grade school youngsters, the impact on the Lamar students has been equally positive. Assistant Principal Porter says that many of those least involved in traditional high school activities have been among those most involved with the Little Vikings. "Many of these kids came to the program with an attitude of 'I'm out for me.' Now they realize that the world doesn't revolve around them. They've learned to give."

For further information, contact
Julie Porter,
Lamar High School, 1400 Lamar Boulevard, Arlington, TX 76012.
Phone: 817-460-4721.

Let's Do Lunch

OLYMPIA, WASHINGTON'S LUNCH BUDDY PROGRAM

The program: Adult volunteers are matched with needy students at local elementary schools. The lunch buddies spend at least one hour a week together, one on one. They eat and then spend the rest of the hour in a variety of activities, such as reading together, playing games, or just talking.

You know that children in your community need all the help they can get. You would like to volunteer at a local school. But you work from nine to five. There's nothing you can do.

But wait! Mary Southon has a question for you: "What are you doing for lunch?"

Mary, the coordinator of volunteer services for the Olympia, Washington, school district, is the force behind the Lunch Buddy program. And if you're a caring person who can give up one lunch hour a week, she would love to pair you with an elementary school student who would benefit from individual adult attention.

You need not despair if you don't happen to live in Olympia. The Lunch Buddy program can be easily implemented in any elementary school district—and it *will* make a difference. Mary tells the story of a second-grader who was not coming to school on Mondays or Fridays. The little girl didn't seem to care about attending, and her mother didn't bother to get her up on those days. The child was paired with a lunch buddy who scheduled her visits for those two days. And suddenly the student started coming on Mondays and Fridays. "She didn't want to miss her buddy," explains Mary, who notes that increased attendance is one of several benefits of the program. "The quality and timeliness of schoolwork has also improved," she says. "The kids show pride in their work, their school, and most important, themselves." Says one fourth-grader in the program, "I don't know what it is, but I just feel so complete now. . . . I guess having a lunch buddy makes me feel that way."

Olympia's program has won national recognition, but it almost didn't get off the ground when conceived in the late 1980s by district administrators. Given the responsibility for finding local businesspeople willing to spend lunch hours in the schools, Mary first approached Olympia's business clubs. Most members responded that they were too busy. She was contemplating her next move when a group of state employees approached her. Several men and women working in the office of the superintendent of public instruction were looking for a volunteer opportunity. "Let's do lunch," said Mary.

The program is not complicated. Carefully screened, caring adults spend at least one lunch hour a week with the same student buddy. The students have been identified by their teachers as needing some extra adult attention and positive recognition. Most often the students are not those with severe behavioral problems but those who are shy and reticent and have difficulty initiating friendships with other children Parental permission is required. "Most parents recognize the wonderful opportunity being offered their children and grant permission with enthusiasm," says Mary.

After eating together, the lunch buddies may read, work on an art project, play a board game, go out to the playground, or just talk. The object of the program is not to provide tutoring but to provide a nonjudgmental friend to a child who needs one. The Lunch Buddy program has been so successful that other schools are investigating implementing similar programs that focus on different populations of children, such as academically talented students.

At present, about eighty volunteers participate at three Olympia elementary schools. The buddies include employees from several state offices, Rotary Club members, and retired people. Most do not have their own children at home. Mary recruits and screens the volunteers and, with the help of the principals and school counselors, trains them and makes the proper matches. Training includes everything from learning school rules to establishing expectations of confidentiality. Adult buddies cannot talk out of school about their students.

Mary emphasizes that for the program to work, "it must be completely welcome by principal and staff." The program does require work and planning on the part of teachers and office personnel, who must make sure that buddies are notified of absences or changes in schedule. There is also interaction between teachers and volunteers who seek advice on how to work with a child. What questions do volunteers most frequently ask? Says Mary, "They end up falling in love with the student and want to know if they can buy them something special." The official response is that anything other than an inexpensive, token gift is not appropriate. But Mary, who is a lunch buddy herself, knows of at least one participant who bought a wardrobe for her financially strapped student.

School districts that are low on funds are increasingly seeking to form partnerships with local businesses. The districts seek monetary support for programs and the participation of employee volunteers. In some communities there are no large corporations to sustain the traditional types of partnerships. In addition, many businesses are on shaky financial footing themselves and cannot afford to give would-be volunteers the time off. But there is a way to give working adults a chance to help without taking away from work or family. The phrase "power lunch" has taken on a new and welcome meaning, thanks to a community's school district and caring citizens.

Mary Southon and the Lunch Buddy program can be contacted at 1113 Legion Way SE, Olympia, WA 98501.
Phone: 206-753-8995.

Peer Pleasure

SHIPLEY'S CHOICE BUDDY-BUDDY PROGRAM

The program: Able-bodied students volunteer to spend time in the lunchroom, classroom, and playground with fellow classmates who have disabilities.

When he was in sixth grade, Denis Brokke volunteered for the Buddy-Buddy program at Shipley's Choice Elementary School in Millersville, Maryland. After screening, training, and orientation, he was paired with a developmentally disabled classmate. The following year Denis had to write an English class composition on the time in his life when he felt best about himself. His thoughts describe the mutual benefits of the program better than any journalist or academic professional can.

Last year when I was in sixth grade I joined a group called Buddy-Buddy Program. I didn't think that was fun at first because I felt weird being around special kids like Down syndrome. These kids were very special at my school the last few years. When it was time to choose my buddy, I chose a boy with Down syndrome. I chose him because he rode my bus and we were friends. My bus driver and I taught him things on the bus like adding single numbers and how to count to twenty. He was a very nice kid.

Throughout the school year we spent a lot of time together like talking and putting the flag up. He loved to play with me. I ate lunch with him whenever I had the chance. I would walk with him and talk with him. Those were the fun things I did with him.

The experience of Denis and more than 170 other student volunteers matched with disabled classmates at Shipley's Choice one day a week demonstrates that special friends do not have to come from outside the school, or limit their contact to lunchtime. Buddies not only eat together but spend time with each other in class and at recess. The results have been heartening and should inspire the growing number of schools that are now mainstreaming physically and mentally challenged children, says Lynne W. Friend, a teacher who created the program when the school district announced that it was moving students from a special school for those with disabilities to Shipley's Choice. A speech therapist, Lynne was familiar with the needs and potential of youngsters with physical or mental difficulties. She approached her principal, who quickly endorsed the idea. Parents of able-bodied and disabled students were equally enthusiastic—with good reason.

Brought into the normal flow of the school, the students with disabilities are happier and demonstrate much higher self-esteem, says Lynne, who now coordinates the program. She adds that the able-bodied students have learned responsibility and gained a better understanding of fellow students who are hearing-impaired, autistic, or have Down syndrome. Most important, lasting friendships that exist beyond school have been formed.

How does Buddy-Buddy work? At the beginning of the year, teachers tell students about the program and give them the opportunity to volunteer. Those who sign up are counseled on the particular needs of their buddies and the kinds of activities that would be most fun and productive—sharing lunch, playing together on the playground, working on a school project. Lynne monitors the program throughout the year and meets regularly with the students to assess progress.

Most students who participate reach the same conclusion Denis did: "I have had many experiences that made me feel good, but never one like this. I've learned a lesson from this experience never to make fun of anyone with Down."

For more information, contact
Lynne W. Friend,
Shipley's Choice Elementary School,
310 Governor Stone Parkway, Millersville, MD 21108.
Phone: 410-987-2506.

13.
IN THE COMMUNITY

Lessen's Plan

G. W. HEWLETT HIGH SCHOOL AND REACHOUT TO SENIORS

The program: Under the auspices of their high school, students perform minor repairs and special services for persons over sixty-five years old.

The image of older Americans has changed dramatically over the past several years. No longer do we think of frail, senile elders whose active, productive lives suddenly cease when they become "senior citizens." Instead, we generally envision fit, sharp men and women who remain busy whether on the job or in retirement. Indeed, as noted elsewhere in this book, many begin second careers as volunteers in their communities. These people live on their own and pride themselves on their independence. Still, there are times when even these vibrant folks can use a helping hand.

Enter G. W. Hewlett High School's Reachout to Seniors, a simple program that could easily be replicated in schools across the country to make a big difference in the lives of older Americans, and younger ones too.

Reachout to Seniors is the brainchild of David Lessen, now a student at the University of Virginia. While in high school in Hewlett, New York, David often visited the travel agency where his mother worked. There he became friendly with two senior citizens who also worked at the agency. These people would periodically lament that they were no longer able to perform certain household chores. Climbing up a ladder to change a light bulb was now difficult, as was turning over a mattress, moving furniture, opening stuck windows, and a wide range of other tasks they had once taken for granted. "These were active people," David says. "They still worked, played golf, and traveled. They just had problems with certain things around the house."

If the person had family living in the area, such problems were easily solved by a visit from a son, daughter, or grandchild. Otherwise, David learned from his friends, the problems were quite costly. An electrician might charge $30 or $40 to come and change a light bulb. Handymen were also expensive, hard to find, and a source of anxiety to those wary of letting strangers into their homes.

Those who knew David had no difficulty opening their doors to him. His offer to help with minor chores at no charge was quickly accepted by his friends at the travel agency. Their lives were obviously the better for his visits, and David found that his was, too. "Most of the stuff I did took only five minutes, and I'd leave feeling great. I knew I'd made them happy and helped them feel like they could continue to be independent."

A light bulb went off in David's head. Why couldn't he organize a program to help older folks in the area with household chores? And why couldn't such an organization be based in his high school? The school would obviously be the largest source of youthful volunteers. Moreover, a school-sanctioned program would have instant credibility. Finally, perhaps the school would provide administrative and financial assistance, doing such things as answering phones and paying for printed material.

David is a logical young man. The steps he took in establishing what he quickly named Reachout to Seniors were carefully conceived, and serve as a primer to students interested in starting similar programs in their communities. He first sought and gained the support of his parents. Then he drafted a proposal for a pilot program and presented it to his principal, Dr. Donald Robbins. The proposal was brief: students would be matched with elderly people in the community who needed someone to do the minor repairs and services David had been providing on his own. There would be no charge for the work done, save for the cost of any materials. Individuals over sixty-five who lived alone or with their spouse and did not have younger family members living nearby were eligible, regardless of their financial status. Seniors would be asked to limit repair sessions to approximately one hour.

"Dr. Robbins was very enthusiastic," David recalls. "He told me that I had my thoughts together. He said he would help me, but that he was going to give me free rein."

There were some restrictions. The program would operate within the boundaries of the school district, and students would not be permitted to perform activities that might lead to liability problems, such as driving the seniors.

Despite the grant of free rein, David had no intention of trying to solve the world's problems overnight. Preliminary research revealed that there were about 1,500 people over the age of sixty-five in the district. Uncertain how many of these would request services and unsure how many of Hewlett High's approximately 1,000 students would volunteer and stay with the program, David did not want to begin by making promises he could not keep. "I wanted to start small so I could see how it was going to work," he says. He decided to establish a pilot program serving only those affiliated with the nearby Five Town Senior Citizen Center This would allow for centralized communication, and at the same time the center could screen those requesting help so that student volunteers could be assured that the homes they visited were safe. David approached the center administrators, who responded positively, offering to run an article about the effort in the center newsletter, providing space for posters about the program, and inviting David to speak about it.

In January 1989, David began his reach-out effort at the center and the high school. At Hewlett he arranged for homeroom teachers to distribute printed material describing the program and inviting potential volunteers to an organizational meeting. Every student received the sheets, which were in question-and-answer format. Sign-up sheets were also placed on school bulletin boards, and David and Dr. Robbins announced the effort over the school public address system.

David was pleasantly shocked by the response. Ninety students returned forms indicating that they were interested in learning more about the program. Thirty classmates showed up for the first meeting, and after David personally contacted others in the school, he had a list of about fifty dependable volunteers.

Seniors from the center were instructed to call the high school, where the operator was to take messages for the program and leave them in a designated box David would then return the calls and arrange for assistance from a team of two students—at least one with a car—whose preferred time to work matched the senior's schedule. After performing the chores, the volunteers would fill out a card indicating what they had done. There was room on the card for any observations or worries about the health or well-being of the client.

The program began in April, but there was just one hitch. Few seniors called. David and his volunteers performed an average of one chore a week until the end of the school year. David, who had wanted to start slow, but not necessarily this slow, admits that the paucity of requests surprised him. Confident that there was a need for the service, he returned to the center to ask people why they weren't calling. They confessed that they were afraid to allow teenagers they didn't know into their homes. "High school students aren't always portrayed that well on television," David says. "We had to overcome that image."

By the time school started in the fall, his senior year, David had a plan to expand the program to the community at large and to overcome the image problem. He visited churches and synagogues to promote Reachout and to allay the fears of older congregation members. He persuaded the public library to promote the effort by displaying brochures, posters, and application forms. And he sent a press release to the local newspapers with the hope that they would write positive articles. Each of these efforts worked, particularly the latter. Once upbeat stories about the efforts of well-meaning teens began appearing, "Things took off," says David.

Serving seniors not associated with the center, which had screened callers, required certain changes. To insure the safety of the student volunteers, who were themselves wary of going into the homes of strangers, David and his mother personally visited those requesting assistance. Faced with this additional responsibility, David delegated some general administrative duties to three reliable friends.

By the time David graduated in the spring of 1990, forty volunteers had gone out on more than one hundred jobs. Chores ranged from hooking up VCRs to hanging curtains, to changing the batteries in smoke detectors, to caulking windows, to putting out patio furniture, which was frequently requested. "A lot of people go away for the winter and need help getting their lawn chairs and tables out in the spring," David explains. He adds that many people who were financially comfortable asked about paying for the students' services. "We told them we would accept minimal donations only to help offset printing costs," says David.

How much time did David put into Reachout to Seniors during his senior year? "Plenty," he acknowledges. "Maybe fifteen or twenty hours per week."

Often programs conceived and driven forward by one enthusiastic leader die when that leader moves on. After David left for college, a group of dedicated students got together to fill his shoes. They kept the program alive but were plagued by the failure of some volunteers to show up at chore sites. All agreed that an adult adviser-coordinator would help. David's mother, Linda, stepped forward to volunteer her services.

Meanwhile, in Charlottesville, Virginia, after getting accustomed to college life, David began a successful Reachout to Seniors program at the university. He coordinates the effort and goes out on jobs. The benefits to the student volunteers equal the benefits to the senior citizens, he insists. "When you talk with older people, you realize how much they've lived through—the Depression, World War II. They can tell you so much more than any textbook can. Unfortunately, none of my living grandparents are nearby. I miss that. This program is the next best thing."

For further information, contact
David Lessen,
c/o G. W. Hewlett High School,
60 Everit Avenue, Hewlett, NY 11557.
Phone: 516-295-3075.

Learning Environment

COAKLEY PROUD CLUB

The program: Students learn the connection between school and real life while participating in academic activities tied to community improvement.

Veteran teacher Gail Thomason heard the same complaint from students every year. "There's no connection between what we do in the classroom and what's happening in the outside world," the young people argued. "Why should we bother to study if what we're supposed to be learning has no application to real life?"

Rather than dismiss these protests as the predictable excuse-making of adolescents, Gail listened. After examining traditional curricula, she concluded that students would indeed try harder and learn more if they saw some relevance in what they were studying.

Gail, who had been a language arts specialist for almost twenty years, admits that this is hardly an earthshaking conclusion. Most teachers realize this, she says. What makes her special is that after reaching the conclusion, she chose to alter radically the way she taught in order to make a difference with her students and in the community at large. Coakley Proud, a club she created in Harlingen, Texas, is a shining example of how students with little interest in their studies can learn to take pride in their schoolwork and better the community while bettering themselves. It is easily replicated in any school where teachers and administrators lament their students' ennui.

When Gail went to the 850-student Coakley Junior High in the late 1980s, she found numerous activities that attracted the school's motivated and gifted students but little to engage the seventy-five seventh- and eighth-graders who were considered at risk of dropping out. It was the time to introduce a program that showed students how what they learned could be useful and have a connection to their lives and the lives of others outside the classroom, she reasoned. She approached Principal Bill Pietro with an idea for a school club that would link community projects to classroom curriculum. Pietro, aware that many of the school's students were turned off by their studies, embraced the idea and gave Gail carte blanche to design her club.

Committed to "turning these kids on to education and to connecting them to the outside world," Gail designed Coakley Proud. Although anyone in the school could participate, her at-risk students became members automatically. They worked on club projects in class and after school thanks to special curricula Gail developed.

Gail began by identifying subjects that might come alive for students under the proper conditions. Since young people were already interested in the environment, she selected ecology as the club's first theme. "I read everything I could get my hands on about the topic and then compiled my own reading and teaching materials," she explains.

Students read and learned about the environment in class and then did something about it outside the classroom. They ran recycling projects, beautified the school campus by picking up litter, cleaned up local beaches, planted flowers in a median strip at a downtown intersection, and wrote letters encouraging government officials to support pro-environmental initiatives. At the same time they sharpened their communication skills by producing books and videos on wildlife, ocean ecology, hazardous wastes, the atmosphere, and energy.

In 1992 Coakley Proud members learned the connection between history—often considered totally irrelevant by students—and their present lives. Gail approached the nearby Rio Grande Valley Museum with an idea for a joint effort to discover and preserve the region's rich Aztec, Mayan, and Spanish past. Highlighting the endeavor was an oral history project. Coakley students interviewed more than three dozen senior citizens, many on camera, to document developments in the valley since the turn of the century. They then produced five books, a slide show, and a videotape that will be used by the museum.

"So many teachers seem just to want to give these kids worksheets to fill up a class period," says Gail. "But if you give them a voice, the results are remarkable. This can be done at any school, anywhere. It just takes leadership."

The benefits to the community are apparent—from flowery median strips to cleaner beaches to sophisticated museum exhibits and historical documents. However, the benefits to the school are even more noticeable; Principal Pietro says that the gap has been bridged between gifted students and the "slower" classmates they once looked down on. The camaraderie students develop while working together on Coakley Proud projects carries over to the rest of the school day, he says.

Coakley Proud has won numerous awards. Most recently, the school won the nationwide Set a Good Example contest, sponsored by the California-based Concerned Businessmen's Association of America. Gail notes that such recognition greatly improves the self-esteem of her students, and she believes that most aren't quite as "at risk" as they once were. "When these kids started, they didn't know the meaning of the word *volunteer.* They wanted to know what was in it for them. They had no conception of helping someone else for nothing. That has all changed," she says proudly.

For more information about Coakley Proud, contact
Gail Thomason,
Route 1, Box 683, Harlingen, TX 78550.

PART 3:

Corporate and
Professional Initiatives

14.
CORPORATE OUTREACH

Research Driven

EASTMAN CHEMICAL COMPANY AND MEALS ON WHEELS

The program: Company employees use flex-time during the workday to deliver hot lunches to homebound participants in the Meals on Wheels program.

Everyone who volunteers in the community has his or her own reason for doing so. Andy Matosky's motivation for mobilizing his fellow workers at Eastman Chemical Company in Kingsport, Tennessee, to form a Meals on Wheels driving team was simple. "My grandmother is the most special person on earth," he explains. "I see her face in the faces of those we're helping. I like to think that if she needed hot meals delivered to her home, there would be somebody there for her."

A 1993 national survey of doctors and nurses revealed that at least one in four older Americans is malnourished. Administrators for home health agencies report an even higher number—44 percent. Meals on Wheels programs throughout the country have long sought to help by engaging community volunteers to deliver warm, nutritious meals to seniors and disabled individuals in need. The efforts of Andy and his fellow employees in Eastman's Research Division is unique because with management's blessing, they use time during the workday to meet this need. Their effort serves as a model for corporations and workers interested in improving their communities.

If not for a bus tour of Kingsport in 1989, the Research Division volunteers may never have taken to their cars. It was on a United Way–sponsored tour of the city that the group learned of a Meals on Wheels waiting list of about fifty elderly and disabled people in Kingsport. "Being naive, I raised my hand and asked how much money it would take to fix the problem," remembers Andy, a research technician in his forties. "I was told that it wasn't money that was needed but drivers."

That started the wheels turning. While still on the bus, Andy asked more questions about how the program worked. Back at the laboratory, he spoke with coworkers who were also interested in figuring out a way to help. By the end of the day about fifteen members of the Research Division said they would volunteer to deliver lunches on their lunch hour if the company would allow it.

But that was a big if, recounts Andy. Delivering the meals would take at least ninety minutes each day, and lunch break at Eastman ran for only one hour. And the company, like most in 1989, had no flex-time provisions that allowed employees to shape their own work hours.

By chance, Andy and others who were interested in creating a Research Division Meals on Wheels team were scheduled to have breakfast the day after the tour with Dr. Jerry Holmes, Eastman's vice president in charge of research. During this meal they told him that they wanted to get involved in Meals on Wheels. They were wary of their chances. "We were told by some that flex-time doesn't just happen," says Andy, who confesses he thought that Holmes would consult higher-ups about permitting employees to adjust hours to accommodate the program. But Holmes gave them the green light. Community service is elementary, he says. "Creating a climate that encourages our people to become involved in volunteer projects they feel strongly about is one way of recognizing their worth to the company and the community."

The deal was simple: employees who used more than the sixty minutes allotted for lunch either could make up time by coming in earlier or staying later or would not be compensated for the additional minutes away from the job. Holmes then threw in another incentive. He would allow Andy to recruit and communicate with volunteers through Eastman's electronic mail system. "This is the only expense to the company," says Andy, "and it's a huge help to us. I can send a message to 150 people with one keystroke on the computer."

Within one week of this breakfast meeting, more than 50 of the 780 workers in the Research Division had volunteered to deliver lunches. Meals on Wheels was delighted, and the process of setting up a program began. Andy and his coworkers Cris Moorehouse and Lisa

Templeton stepped forward to organize the program. Their responsibilities included forming twenty-five two-person driving teams, scheduling the teams, working with the Meals on Wheels driver coordinator, Mary Cunningham, to set up routes, and making maps and leading dry runs on the routes so the volunteers could accomplish their tasks quickly and efficiently.

The program was officially launched about five months after Andy raised his hand on the bus trip around Kingsport. Each weekday morning two driving teams left the workplace between 10:30 and 11:00, picked up meals, delivered them to sixteen to twenty-two people on the route, and returned to work between noon and 12:30. Because there were twenty-five teams, volunteers were required to drive only one or two days each month—a relatively small sacrifice resulting in a large collective result. Eighteen months after the program began, another twenty employees had signed on, and the company picked up another Meals on Wheels route.

Thanks to electronic mail and team spirit, Andy is quickly able to find substitutes if a scheduled driver is unable to keep his or her commitment on a given day. "I've never had anyone turn down a last-minute request," he says. "I've called a lab coordinator ten minutes before it was time to leave, and he was willing to go."

What is involved in delivering a meal to a particular Meals on Wheels participant? Many of those served have special needs, notes Andy. For example, a woman with arthritis may need to have her milk not only delivered but opened and placed in a particular position. Volunteers note that the daily personal contact they provide seems as essential to the homebound people as the lunch itself. Occasionally, those delivering the food will come upon a person who has fallen or taken ill and is in need of immediate help. There are instructions on how to meet such emergencies.

As is often the case with such initiatives, the relationship between the volunteers and those they serve often extends beyond the brief lunchtime visit. Discovering that one elderly participant's driveway had become inaccessible because of potholes, the Research Division team spent a weekend repaving it with materials purchased by team members. On another weekend, the team worked with a local church group to build a ramp at the home of a disabled veteran. The team has also enlisted Boy Scout troops and other volunteers to help those on the route with household chores. "The synergy in this kind of effort is magical," says Andy.

He adds that the people on the Meals on Wheels route are not the only ones nourished by the Eastman employees' initiative. Morale and camaraderie in the Research Division has increased as "we get to know our fellow workers better." Equally important, the hunger of many to do something meaningful in the community has been satisfied. "Growing up, my generation was out to change the world," says Andy. "But then, as we got older, it all seemed so hard. Now I realize that I really can make a difference."

> For further information, contact the
> Meals on Wheels or United Way affiliate in your community or
> Andy Matosky,
> Eastman Chemical Company, P.O. Box 511, Kingsport, TN 37662.

World of Difference

CHRYSLER CORPORATION'S WORLD OF WORK

> **The program:** Employees are linked with specific public schools to prepare today's children for tomorrow's workplace. Volunteers are given time during the workday to tutor, act as mentors, and lead activities that help students develop personal responsibility, regular attendance, creativity, and teamwork.

When former Saginaw, Michigan, teacher and principal Valerie Becker wrote Lee Iacocca an unsolicited letter in 1989, she was uncertain whether the busy Chrysler Corporation chairman would respond. She certainly didn't expect him to invite her to a meeting in his offices at Chrysler headquarters in Detroit. And she had no idea that he would eventually hire her to develop and coordinate an ambitious effort to demonstrate that corporate America could make an impact in our public schools. "This whole thing is serendipity," she marvels.

The unpredictable turn of events began when Valerie took pen to paper after reading Iacocca's two books and several columns he had written for the *Detroit Free Press* about the sorry state of American education. "I'm a zealot on this subject," confesses Valerie, who at the time was a consultant on fine arts and gifted learning programs to the Dearborn, Michigan, school system. In a three-paragraph letter, Valerie told the chairman that educators alone were not responsible for the fact that students were graduating from high school without the skills to succeed in life in general and the workplace in particular. "I wrote that society and parents had to take some responsibility," Valerie remembers. "I said that some parents simply weren't aware of their children's needs. They dropped their kids off at kindergarten, picked them up when they were through with twelfth grade, and expected the school to have done everything."

The surprise phone call from Iacocca's office came within days. Could Valerie meet with the chairman to discuss her thoughts about education? Of course, she said, stunned. When the shock wore off, she "called everyone I knew in the field to get their ideas. I set up focus groups. I didn't want to go in just representing myself," she says.

Armed with a number of ideas, Valerie appeared at Chrysler on the appointed day to counsel one of the most visible and powerful leaders in America. (Her first thoughts on meeting Iacocca: "He was taller than I expected.") Two other educators, both men, had also been invited. Mr. Iacocca asked each of his three guests to speak for five minutes on what corporate America could do to improve the public schools. He then responded to their arguments and asked each to summarize his or her position in a one-minute statement. (Valerie's next thoughts on meeting Iacocca: "I was impressed that he didn't presume that he knew everything. He was genuinely interested in finding out what we thought worked.")

At the end of the presentations, Iacocca asked his guests to send him letters inviting him to the schools in which they worked. He would select one and visit for a day. While Valerie thought she had made the best presentation, she did not expect him to visit a school in Dearborn. "That's where Ford is headquartered," she explains. But a few days after sending her letter, she received a call saying that the chairman would like to go to school with her. And he did, spending a full day visiting classes, talking with teachers, and soliciting her views on education.

A few days later, Iacocca offered Valerie a job. She was unaware that the company had been conducting a nationwide search for a national education program administrator, an individual who could develop a corporate initiative in the public schools. The job description suggested that she would be a consultant to Chrysler for a year. "I was leery," she confesses. "I wasn't sure I wanted to give up my job in Dearborn—who knew if I could get it back after a year?—so I asked if I could take a leave of absence." When the school district consented, she accepted Chrysler's offer. She started in July 1989 and has been there ever since, having been made a full-time employee after twelve months.

Lee Iacocca, one of America's most outspoken capitalists, may be surprised to learn that Valerie "felt like I was in Russia at first." The differences between the cultures of a public school with dozens of employees and a minimum of red tape and a publicly held company with tens of thousands of workers and the attendant bureaucracy were enormous. In addition, Valerie wasn't sure whether she was considered anything more than a frill by many executives, whose main concern was to produce automobiles.

Chrysler had long been involved in helping colleges by providing training programs, scholarships, and other financial support. But Iacocca had concluded what executives at Xerox and a handful of other major corporations had concluded: America's future workforce was dropping out of school before entering college, or coming out of high school so ill-prepared for the workplace that intervention was needed long before college. Valerie's mandate was simple. "Mr. Iacocca told me to do something that gets our employees involved, that doesn't cost a lot of money." She explains that because the automobile business is so unpredictable and cyclical, the company was reluctant to commit funding to new programs it might not be able to support after start-up.

As a principal in Saginaw, Valerie had tried to persuade community members to come to her school and share their talents. Surveying the scene in Chrysler's hometown, Detroit, she became even more convinced that people from the community were needed in the schools. "Many urban children have never known a relative who worked," she says. "They first have to learn what a job is and what it takes to hold one." World of Work was designed to help these children grasp the relationship between school and work. "Attitudes learned in school will help students keep a job when they enter the workforce," Valerie says. What kind of attitudes? Awareness of the importance of daily attendance, job completion, and responsible behavior. Such awareness helps develop effective educational tools as well, says Valerie. And who can instill such attitudes? Employee volunteers who spend time on a regular schedule with elementary school students.

Valerie believes in starting small. She first contacted Florence McMurtry, the dynamic principal of Glazer Elementary School, an inner-city school just a few blocks from Chrysler's headquarters. Location was important. To meet normal classroom schedules, volunteers would be taking time off during the workday. The less travel time they had to put in, the better.

Principal McMurtry was interested. She detailed the needs of her school and invited Valerie to visit. Mutually beneficial goals should be developed by the corporation and the principal before the program is presented to the teachers and staff at the school, advises Valerie. After making her presentation at Glazer, Valerie found some of the teachers less than enthusiastic. At first they were wary that outsiders were coming in to do their jobs. Valerie explained that World of Work was a volunteer program designed not to supplant the teachers but to provide assistance and bring something different to the students. She convinced them to give the program a try and returned to her office with requests for eight volunteers.

These volunteers would be chosen very carefully, says Valerie. Screening was most important, because the employees would be dealing with impressionable, often vulnerable children and because they were representing the corporation in the community. Valerie put a notice in the *Chrysler Times,* an internal publication that reaches all employees. The notice explained that she was looking for people who had experience working with children. The employees must be willing to commit at least one hour per week to visiting the school. The company would grant them release time, but they would be expected to fulfill all of their responsibilities at work. Valerie then conducted personal interviews with those who wanted to volunteer. The eight who were chosen received extensive training in such things as the learning characteristics of children, specific school policies, and behavior management. Training for all new volunteers remains a requirement today.

The first World of Work program, instituted at Glazer in January 1990, was the establishment of a math pentathlon team. This was followed by the creation of a debate society, which attracted fifty children interested in discussing contemporary issues. These efforts were so successful that several more teachers at the school requested Chrysler volunteers.

Having created a successful relationship between one school and employees at one Chrysler site, Valerie moved forward. Bernard Robertson, the vice president of the Jeep and Truck Division, was an early supporter of the World of Work concept. Soon two additional Detroit schools were being served by employees he helped recruit. "Then it just grew and grew and grew," says Valerie. Now more than two thousand Chrysler employees at more than fifty sites around the country are working in local schools. They tutor, start clubs, teach new skills, serve as role models, and "guide youngsters toward a career path of responsibility and success," Valerie explains.

Of course, a volunteer who puts in an hour or two with a child each week is no substitute for a parent. Each school therefore hosts a Getting to Know You Night for parents, to introduce the World of Work program and to encourage parents to join the volunteer effort. The results have been encouraging. Chrysler, which has several educational initiatives in addition to World of Work, also publishes a brochure that explains how parents can help their children succeed in school.

World of Work has met both of the goals Iacocca established at the outset. Large numbers of employees are now involved in the public schools, and the program, while labor-intensive, is not costly. "It could be replicated at minimal expense by any corporation," Valerie says. But to succeed, she adds, such a program needs to focus on a particular issue, such as education, and it requires the support and leadership of the company's top executives.

In addition to setting the wheels in motion for the creation of a better workforce as the twenty-first century approaches, Chrysler has seen an improvement in its current workforce thanks to the program. The volunteers have shown personal growth that carries over to their job performance. Although this was not an objective of the program, it does help sell it to the company, says Valerie.

The volunteers themselves do not need to be sold. Valerie recalls a rally held at the beginning of the past school year: "I heard one of our employees saying, 'I can't wait to get back to the classroom and get those hugs.'"

For further information, contact
Valerie Becker, National Education Program Administrator,
Chrysler Corporation,
12000 Chrysler Drive, Highland Park, MI 48288-1919.
Phone: 313-956-0607.

Branching Out

BARNETT BANK OF JACKSONVILLE'S COMMUNITY INVOLVEMENT PROGRAM

The program: Each of the bank's branches annually adopts its own community not-for-profit organization, and employees become involved in hands-on activities.

Hugh Jones, Jr., the chairman of Barnett Bank of Jacksonville, is fond of quoting an old saying: *Tell me and I will forget. Show me and I may remember. But involve me and I will understand.* Since 1983, Barnett Bank's eight hundred employees have been involved in a wide range of activities that have allowed them to understand the people and issues in their Florida community better and to create positive change in the lives of thousands of the area's citizens. In 1992 alone, volunteers from all thirty-four Barnett branches and every support department gave more than forty thousand hours of direct service to more than forty groups under the Barnett Community Involvement Program—a program that can be replicated by any bank or other business with multiple branches or locations.

The projects have been as varied as the Barnett employees who have selected them. Staffers from the downtown bank cook dinner once a week for families who are staying at the local Ronald McDonald House while their children are receiving treatment at area hospitals. Employees at the San Jose branch hold an annual Christmas party for children with leukemia. The Corporate Services Department adopted a local family, providing legal assistance, home upkeep, transportation, moral support, and love to a terminally ill mother and her three sons.

What inspired Hugh Jones to initiate such an ambitious program? Sadly, he was moved by a 1982 airplane crash that killed the top officials of Jacksonville's Charter Corporation. After reading newspaper stories about the volunteer work that these executives and other Charter employees had performed to renovate residences for senior citizens, the Barnett chairman decided to see whether bank employees could be organized to volunteer in hands-on projects that met community needs.

He started small. Conversations with people at Volunteer Jacksonville, which matches volunteers with needy groups, revealed that the Transient Youth Center required assistance. Soon employees from Barnett's San Jose branch were working individually with the troubled teenagers residing at the center. "The success of this activity insured that volunteering would become a part of the corporate culture," says Judy Hall, who as Barnett's vice president for community affairs coordinates the program.

Judy credits two factors for the expansion and continued success of the program over the past ten years. First, she says, Hugh Jones's leadership and enthusiasm have been essential. "The commitment to caring must start at the top, with the CEO. If you have that, the caring at the grass-roots level will follow and keep the effort alive." Second, she cites "a real healthy lack of structure." While inspiration comes from the top, specific directives do not. Each branch determines which group it will adopt and what it will do for the group. "That leads to a greater feeling at the branches that 'we did this; this is ours,' " Judy explains.

Usually a committee within a branch determines what the program will be and checks with Judy. Then one person steps forward to take charge. "Sometimes it's the branch manager, but more often it's a teller or secretary or junior executive," Judy says. She adds that several employees have demonstrated such leadership in coordinating their branch's programs that they have been rewarded with greater responsibilities and opportunities for advancement at work.

Does the bank's bottom line suffer from the time given to not-for-profit groups? Absolutely not, says Judy. "Our attitude is that we have commitments to our customer and to our community, and that each branch can figure out how to achieve those. I've never seen evidence that the bottom line has suffered." She notes that the healthier the economic and social climate is in Jacksonville, the greater the chances are that business in general and the bank in particular will thrive. Also, the program creates stronger morale in the workplace and allows employees to get to know one another better—additional factors that lead to increased productivity.

Like Hugh Jones, Judy is convinced that donating a little part of one's paycheck to charity each month is admirable, but donating one's time is the key to personal growth and bettering the community. "Once people absorb this, they're not likely to abandon it," she says. "They grab hold of it for the rest of their lives. Few people can reject the value they receive from doing something for someone else."

For further information, contact
Judy Hall, V.P. Community Affairs,
Barnett Bank of Jacksonville,
P.O. Box 990, Jacksonville, Florida 32231.
Phone: 904-791-7427.

Insuring the Future

ITT HARTFORD'S SKILLS TRAINING ADVANCEMENT GROUP

The program: A corporation's work-study program gives high school juniors the opportunity to combine office skills training and academic enrichment with on-the-job experience.

The social unrest of the mid-sixties moved many corporations to become more involved in their communities. In 1966, Connecticut-based ITT Hartford, then known as the Hartford Insurance Group, launched a temporary program designed to keep a group of young men from the inner city off the streets for the summer. With counselors and material provided by the company, the youths restored a rundown summer camp in Moodus, Connecticut. The success of this badly needed one-time project moved a group of Hartford Group employees to meet with city leaders and design the Skills Training Advancement Group (STAG), an ongoing program that would last beyond the long hot sum-

mer and, in the words of company officials, "provide greater and potentially more lasting benefits to the young people of Hartford."

The conferees determined that students from poor neighborhoods
would benefit most from an opportunity to develop occupational skills
and improve academic skills. As one of the major companies in the city,
the Hartford Group had a wealth of talented employees who could lend
expertise and direction to teens moving on to college or entering the
labor force. This could best be accomplished through a work-study
program that provided high school juniors with special training in language, math, and business skills and steady paid work with the company over the school year. The idea was sound in 1966 and remains
sound today. Over the past three decades, STAG has helped more than
one thousand students prepare for a successful future.

How does it work? During their sophomore year, students at Hartford's three public high schools are given the opportunity to apply for
the forty-five openings in the work-study program. Typically, about a
hundred students apply. Working with the schools, the company then
selects participants, who divide their junior year between the school and
the workplace, where they are assigned to a particular ITT Hartford
department.

Many American businesses, large and small, offer young people the
chance to work during the school year. To insure its students' success in
the program and the real world, STAG goes one step further. In addition to on-the-job training, participants receive instruction in English,
mathematics, and business communication skills during an intense
eight-week summer program. Once the school year begins, the students
also have an opportunity to improve their public speaking through an
association with the toastmasters' organization, earn college credits from
Greater Hartford Community College, and compete for college scholarships.

Does such training prepare the STAG students for the real world?
ITT Hartford thinks so. More than 20 percent of the program participants remain with the company after graduating from high school or
college. Success stories abound. For example, Kris Sawyer worked in the
claims department as a member of STAG's class of 1972. Today she is a
senior claims representative in the company's Workers' Compensation
Division.

Many STAG graduates who find work outside the corporation

attribute their success to skills developed in the work-study program. Emory Wilson, class of 1984, says he learned how to use a computer and to communicate clearly over the phone, skills essential to his current work as a pharmacist.

Quentin Gleason, a college student, also learned to use a computer. But he is most grateful for lessons less tangible. "I learned a lot about how you have to act in the business world, about the importance of punctuality, how you're expected to dress, and how to communicate. It's a program that gives people a rare kind of opportunity."

For further information, contact
Sandra Sharr, Director of Community Affairs,
ITT Hartford, Hartford Plaza, Hartford, CT 06115.
Phone: 203-547-4972.

A Catalog of Ideas

BIOBOTTOMS

> **The program:** A company promotes community involvement through its catalog by identifying worthy local not-for-profit organizations as examples of grass-roots creativity.

Biobottoms sells "fresh-air wear for kids" and accessories through catalogs that make it clear that children hold the future, not just for the company but for all of us. The business, based in Petaluma, California, has devised an ingenious yet remarkably simple way of using its mailings to encourage volunteerism. Easily replicable by any catalog company, this approach has the potential to inspire millions of citizens to become involved.

Biobottoms' fall 1993 catalog, distributed to over four million households, spotlighted "Eight 'Do-Gooder' Groups That Make a Difference," briefly describing each organization's activities and providing mailing addresses. Why? In a note to customers, founders Joan Cooper and Anita Dimondstein reasoned that since most of the company's customers are the parents of young children, they "tend to be pro-peace, pro-child, pro-health care, pro-environment, and pro-education." To inspire this already receptive audience to become a part of the volunteer movement, Joan and Anita decided to "put some catalog space to work for eight energetic, innovative organizations that we've gotten to know." Thus, while browsing through pages selling everything from wool diaper covers to varsity jackets, readers also got to know about groups that offer the homeless meaningful jobs, promote arts in the schools, involve children in environmental and wildlife preservation, and provide emotional support to those with AIDS. The selection of these organizations was not haphazard. Joan and Anita or others at Biobottoms were either involved or familiar with all of them.

Biobottoms' own involvement in the community reflects the sensibilities of the founders, who came of age in the 1960s. The company, which was started in 1981 to distribute Japanese-made all-wool covers for cloth diapers and now boasts annual sales of over $15 million, is a member of Businesses for Social Responsibility and the Business Partnership for Peace and donates a percentage of profits to promote world harmony. It has also given clothing to the needy around the world and has sponsored a village bank in Guatemala that provides capital to poor Third World women to start small businesses. Joan and Anita say the Biobottoms line is simple: "It seems like we're all going to have to be active and involved in order to confront the problems that face our communities today." Those selling products through catalogs can help by promoting volunteerism as well.

For further information, contact
Biobottoms,
617C Second Street, Petaluma, CA 94952.
Phone: 707-778-7168.

15.
PROFESSIONAL OUTREACH

Quid Pro Quo

DONALD HORTON AND OPERATION UPLIFT

The program: Clients receiving free legal services are asked to do volunteer work in their community for the same number of hours that the lawyer worked for them. Thus, lawyers who work pro bono can multiply the effects of their efforts in the community.

When Marcy Ellert asked Minneapolis attorney Don Horton how much she owed him for an hour's worth of advice on an employment discrimination matter, he winced. "She was the daughter of a friend of mine, and a student, so I didn't want to charge her at all," he recalls. Don, who specializes in the civil rights area, had counseled Marcy that she probably didn't have a case. Still, the young woman wanted to pay him something. The lawyer thought for a moment, and "then I told her to go down to the food bank in her neighborhood and volunteer her time for an hour, since that's how long I worked for her, and I would consider her bill paid," he says.

Presenting this ad hoc suggestion, Don had no notion that he was laying the groundwork for a program that would enable lawyers—and other professionals—to increase their ability to make a difference in the community dramatically . . . with very little time, expense, or paperwork. That, however, is the simple beauty of Operation Uplift.

Don says he never expected what happened after Marcy left his office. "She returned two weeks later and told me that she had spent three hours at the food bank and intended to go back again. She said that what I had done had changed her views about volunteering and lawyers for the better."

Don was moved by Marcy's words and actions. He started thinking that there might be others who would be interested in doing volunteer or community service work in exchange for legal services. Some of these people were indigent, while others, like Marcy, were friends or family members whom lawyers felt they could not charge.

"I talked with other attorneys who do pro bono work," Don says. "They told me that often their pro bono clients wanted to do something for them. None of the attorneys would accept any money, but they all thought that allowing clients to square the account by volunteering would give many a sense of dignity they might not otherwise feel."

This positive informal market research inspired Don to establish Operation Uplift in 1989. One doesn't have to be a rocket scientist, or even an attorney, to understand the concept. When a lawyer decides to represent a client who cannot afford legal representation, the client is asked to do volunteer work in his or her community. Clients who agree to sign Operation Uplift agreements promise to volunteer their services for the same number of hours that their attorney spends working on their case. Each month the attorney sends the client a letter stating how much time was spent on his or her case. The client then performs that many hours of volunteer work.

The clients can choose their own form of service. They can help a neighbor or a community group such as a food bank, or they can volunteer through their place of worship or any volunteer service organization. When clients have finished their volunteer work, they send the attorney a confirmation of payment, which is usually just a letter telling about their experience.

What if a client fails to perform the volunteer services? There are no consequences, says Don. "The important thing is that many clients *will* live up to the agreement, and a tremendous number of people will be helped by the ripple effect of Operation Uplift." There is no minimum number of Operation Uplift clients that a lawyer must accept, and pro bono clients do not have to participate. "It's recommended," says Don, "but always a matter of free choice."

To turn the ripple into a wave, Don has sent Operation Uplift agreements, sample letters, and instruction sheets to the American Bar Association and the bar associations in all fifty states. The associations are asked to distribute the materials free to interested lawyers. He has since heard from many lawyers across the country who have had their own successful Operation Uplift exchanges.

What does the program mean to a community? Don proudly shows before-and-after pictures of a dilapidated house turned beautiful by one of his pro bono clients, who supervised and helped a group of students paint it. Another client spent a day picking up trash with a group of volunteers in a state park. And another organized a church group to prepare and serve dinner for sixty people at a downtown shelter. "I spent approximately five hours on the project and purchased the food," the client wrote Don. "This was a very eye-opening experience for myself and for those who participated. . . . Operation Uplift has caused several of us to get involved."

Don says that Operation Uplift does not need to be limited to lawyers. Doctors and others providing free services could easily adapt the program to their professions. He concludes, "When you take the time to help or lift up someone, you are affirming their intrinsic worth as human beings. The message we want to send to people is, not only are you worth helping, but you have something to give to others. Operation Uplift asks people to look at themselves and ask what they can do to help others."

Operation Uplift has no meetings, officers, or dues. It is free for participating law firms. Agreements and sample letters should be available from state bar associations and the American Bar Association.

For further information, contact
Operation Uplift,
c/o Horton and Associates, 700 Title Insurance Building,
400 Second Avenue South, Minneapolis, MN 55401.

The Patients of a Saint

DR. DINIA CRUZ AND THE CRUZ MOBILE CLINIC

The program: A pediatrician turns a van into a traveling doctor's office, taking medical care to the doorsteps of poor families living in public housing projects.

Shortly after pediatrician Dinia Cruz began paying house calls at Memphis housing projects in her mobile medical van, she was approached by a fellow doctor whom she greatly respected. "Why don't you go to East Memphis, where the rich people live, so you don't have to play Jesus Christ anymore?" he asked. The remark not only stunned Dinia, it offended her. "I wasn't doing it because I wanted to be godly; I wasn't even doing it because it was the right thing to do. It just happened."

But how? Why would a pediatrician with the opportunity to take care of rich patients who paid their bills on time choose to visit less-than-safe neighborhoods and serve those who were either unable to pay or on Medicaid, which is often slow to pay and involves entering a bureaucratic maze?

For Dinia, the reason was simple: "I saw a need." She adds that she may have been predisposed to help the disadvantaged because of her own background as an immigrant. After growing up and studying medicine in the Philippines, she came to the United States, in 1976. Two years at the County Health Department in Memphis further sensitized her to the problems of the indigent.

When Dinia established her private practice in Memphis in 1983, she set up an office in the eastern part of Memphis, where she served primarily middle-class patients. She also kept regular hours at a hospital in another part of the city. "I hadn't even realized there was a public housing project with three hundred units close by," she confesses. Many of the residents, most of whom were on Medicaid, became her patients at the hospital's clinic.

In 1985 Dinia discontinued her affiliation with the hospital. Anxious to continue serving her disadvantaged patients, she looked for office space in the neighborhood. In the meantime, she says, "My old patients from the hospital kept calling and asking, 'Where are you, Dr. Cruz?'"

When a deal for an office fell through, the idea for a mobile clinic did indeed "just happen." Dinia explains, "One day I looked at the small van I had and wondered, *Why can't I go to the housing project once a week until I find space?*"

Dinia says that when she posed this question to the Memphis Housing Authority a few days later, "they were a bit wary." After she provided them with references and explained her motives, that wariness turned to enthusiasm. "They asked me if I could go to other housing projects, too." The Housing Authority was well aware that because of a number of factors, many families in the projects rarely saw a doctor or received regular medical care. Convinced that Dinia's proposal was sound, officials introduced her to enthusiastic tenants' councils at most of the city's eighteen housing projects.

Given the green light by the city and the tenants, Dinia abandoned the hunt for a second office and contemplated her own vehicle—a small Chevy van customized for her family. The van was comfortable enough for her husband and two young sons, but could it accommodate patients? Dinia didn't know of any other doctor in the country who used a mobile office, and therefore she literally had to invent the wheels. Although she had determined that she would not need a great deal of equipment, she would require space for a scale, an examining table, chairs, supplies, herself, a nurse, and a driver. It soon became clear that the family van would be too small. Undaunted, the doctor paid a call to a local mobile home dealership and bought a thirty-six-foot van.

Still committed to the patients at her East Memphis office, Dinia decided that she would visit each of the eighteen projects one or two times a month at a regularly scheduled time. No appointments would be necessary; the patients could just walk in. Dinia would focus on children but would also treat their mothers if necessary.

The tenants' associations at each project and the Housing Authority agreed to post fliers announcing her visits and to encourage residents to bring their children for regular checkups or special care. The campaign worked. From the beginning, there was no shortage of patients. Those from the projects whom Dinia had seen at the hospital had obviously sought medical attention before. But many whom she now saw had, she says, fallen through the cracks. One mother brought in five children under the age of seven, none of whom had ever been immunized.

Although most families greeted the van's arrival as enthusiastically as they might greet the local ice cream truck, Dinia wanted to reach everybody. After stationing the van in a designated spot at a housing project, the driver would knock on doors to encourage attendance. To encourage patients to visit again, the doctor would try to make follow-up phone calls, but unfortunately, many people living in the projects were without telephones.

Unable to afford phones, these patients were also unable to afford medical care. In most instances, the Medicaid program reimbursed Dinia. She treated those without Medicaid or other means of payment for free. Sadly, a doctor who relies on Medicaid reimbursement often finds herself forced to deal more with red tape than with adhesive tape. After seven years of filling out government forms, Dinia began to burn out. Unwilling to abandon her housing project patients, however, she cut her van visits from Mondays, Wednesdays, and Fridays to Saturdays only.

There has been an up side to this downscaling. "On the weekend, I can bring my two teenage sons along," she explains. "They go to an exclusive school where almost everybody comes from the same privileged background. I want them to see that there is a different world out there."

Since Dr. Cruz began her mobile van in 1986, several individuals or communities have introduced similar initiatives. Those interested in further information should contact
Dr. Dinia Cruz, Cruz Mobile Clinic,
P.O. Box 770180, Memphis, TN 38177.
Phone: 901-683-9511.

PART 4:
Getting Involved

16.
BOOKS AND BREAKFAST: SHARON FIFFER'S DIARY

Like many mothers who work outside the home, for years I limited my community service to projects at the three different schools of our children—high school, elementary school, and private nursery school. If a child's activity demanded involvement—AYSO soccer, for example, requires all parents to volunteer in some capacity throughout the playing season—Steve and I both did our part. Any volunteer activity that did not directly relate to my own family simply did not fit into my schedule. Yes, I might contribute a small amount of money to what I deemed a worthwhile cause, and yes, I might give change to someone on the street who asked me for it. I donated our used clothes to worthy organizations. But I felt that any community service project that demanded my physical presence and personal energy was something I literally did not have the time for.

How did I get to that place? I had attended a Catholic high school that included community service as a part of our educational requirements. As a teenager, I happily tutored elementary school students, collected and distributed food to the hungry, and washed cars to raise money for charity. As a college student in the late 1960s, I signed petitions for farmworkers, boycotted produce, marched against the Vietnam war, and vowed that when I and my fellow students were in charge, the world would be a different place. I would take the time to do good and change the world.

Then I graduated from college.

Work finally became a career; romance grew into marriage; and having a family meant that everything that did not relate to my babies, my toddlers, my growing students, came in second. Recently, Steve and

I realized that as our children grow and question the world around them, we have to be able to provide practical rather than abstract answers, offer belief systems, and help establish values. It became clear once again that we had to take the wider view—that we had to take the time to do good and change the world.

We knew and admired people who, through their churches, temples, or secular service clubs, made volunteering part of their daily lives and their children's lives. We knew that community service was possible. Since we weren't affiliated with a church or a temple—our respective Jewish and Catholic backgrounds are more part of our cultural identity than of our religious practice—Steve and I began talking about doing something independently. Steve began serving on various community boards—a public interest law firm, the Evanston Arts Council, then the city's Human Relations Commission. I continued to avoid anything that had a committee attached to it. And until Steve heard about the Books and Breakfast program at another Evanston school and it struck a chord in both our heads and our hearts, I continued to state, reluctantly but adamantly, that I simply had no time to volunteer for anything.

The diary that follows demonstrates what I was missing and what I found.

May 11, 1992

Steve ran into Joe Zendell, director of the Evanston Arts Council, who told him about our mutual friend Sue Sussman's involvement in something she was calling Books and Breakfast. Sue is a writer of both adult and children's fiction, and as a children's writer frequently visits local schools.

Joe described her concern about some students who were restless and inattentive. When she talked to teachers and the health clerk, she found out that an alarming number of children arrived at school hungry every morning. These kids would often tell their teachers they didn't feel good, and the teachers would send them to the nurse's office. There, juice, crackers, or any other food on hand would revive them. Their stomach aches and headaches, their restlessness and fatigue, and in some cases even their anger were not necessarily symptoms of illness or a chronic behavior problem. The cause was often hunger. (This is no surprise to teachers, most of whom keep crackers or cookies in their desk, knowing they will have hungry children arriving each morning.)

Sue the mother saw the solution to hungry children fairly quickly: feed them. And Sue the writer saw a way to provide another kind of satisfaction. Why not nourish the mind as well as the body by reading to the children as they ate each morning? Wouldn't this develop a lifelong association between the comfort of a good breakfast and the satisfaction of hearing a wonderful story?

This is the way Steve described his conversation about Sue and the Books and Breakfast program she began at Orrington School about six weeks ago. He hasn't talked to her yet—he wants to know what I think about beginning a similar program at Kingsley Elementary School, where our eight-year-old daughter, Nora, is in second grade. Certainly this is a program that appeals to us on a gut level. Feeding children and reading books to them—who can argue the politics of that? Maybe it's time to put up or shut up.

June 8, 1992

Steve called Sue to get more detailed information about the program. We had talked it over and speculated about who might be willing to start Kingsley Books and Breakfast with us. As usual, we talked ourselves to death without actually seeing the program in action. Sue invited us to visit Orrington School before the school year ended, and we did on this the last day of the program.

Books and Breakfast began as soon as the first bus arrived and ended when the school bell rang—twenty to twenty-five minutes later, maximum. For this last day, Sue had persuaded an editor at *Booklist* to donate new children's books that had been sent to that publication for review. She had individually wrapped these books and planned on handing them out to the children to honor their participation in Books and Breakfast.

We arrived just before the children. Orrington School is surrounded by large homes with well-tended lawns, a few blocks from Lake Michigan. In this almost idyllic setting, right out of a *Leave It to Beaver* episode, how could there be hungry children?

Evanston is the first community north of Chicago, so it has a more urban feel than most North Shore suburbs. It has the lakefront, Northwestern University, a commitment to diversity and integrated schools, and, unlike many suburban communities, an enormous chasm in the socioeconomic status of its residents. Because Evanston has a commitment to racial balance in its schools, busing is a matter of course. Some of the poorest children in the city are bused to Orrington School, in one of the wealthiest neighborhoods. Right or wrong, politics aside, these are some of the children who, by necessity, come to school hungry.

At Orrington, Sue offers up an impressive spread—muffins, bagels, cereal, fruit, milk, and juice. She has paid for this food and the plates and napkins during this "pilot" six weeks, but she hopes to get funds from a state agency or foundation that will reimburse her and support the program next year.

Teachers and parents help serve the food while Sue reads. Today, Orrington Principal Joanne Wilkins attended so she could hand out the book awards to the children at the end of breakfast. Steve and I sat in the back of the crowded art room and watched the children come in, set down their backpacks, and get in line for food. I kept my eye on one small boy, maybe six or seven years old, who filled his plate seemingly beyond capacity. Two muffins, six orange slices, a bagel and cream cheese, a carton of milk—I smiled, thinking that his eyes were bigger than his stomach. Then I watched him eat every scrap of food on that plate as he listened to Sue read a chapter from Roald Dahl's *The Witches.*

These children were not idly taking the food just because it was there—they were hungry. They cleaned their plates, stepped forward to receive their special books, and when the bell rang went off to their classrooms. One girl had a muffin sticking out of her pocket, but no one questioned her. The principal told us that she took it to her brother, a fifth-grader who thought Books and Breakfast was just for the little kids.

We hung around watching the cleanup and ran into the drama teacher, who asked us why we were observing the program. When we told him we were thinking about starting up a similar program at another school, he offered his own endorsement. He told us that although there was probably no way to document the effects of Books and Breakfast accurately, he knew that the benefits trickled throughout the entire day and throughout the entire school.

Some of the kids who were now eating breakfast and listening to a story used to get into fights on the playground—maybe because they were hungry and cranky. And maybe because they now started the day with an adult reading to them rather than yelling at them, they were beginning to enter the classroom readier to learn and cooperate. They benefited, their teachers benefited, and their classmates benefited. The drama teacher was right. It wasn't scientific data. It was anecdotal evidence—and plenty good enough for us.

June 12, 1992

We called our good friend Judy Groothuis, who besides being actively involved in PTA activities is the mother of Nora's best friend, Elizabeth. If we are actually going to undertake this program, our daughters will have to play active roles as well. We described the program sketchily, asking if Judy would be willing to help coordinate if we got the okay to begin a Kingsley Books and Breakfast. Yes, she said, without a moment's hesitation. It pays to have good friends and to know which ones to ask to participate in which projects.

Judy is a natural for this. A nurse who is working part-time so she can be on call for her two daughters, she had an immediate response to hungry children: "Let's feed them." She volunteered to call another Kingsley parent, Lauren Paulson, who she thought would be interested. We told Judy we would get more details from Sue, then meet with her and Lauren. Then we'd all meet with Dr. Mike Martin, the principal of Kingsley School.

June 30, 1992

Steve talked to Sue. Emotionally we understand the problem and what we think is a partial solution, but what about the mechanics? How do we determine which children are the hungry ones? How do we fund the program? Where do we get our volunteers? What about the logistics of getting the food prepared and served?

With Orrington as our model program, we don't need to reinvent the wheel, but we do need information. Gail Brodsky, the Orrington PTA president, dropped off a packet about the program earlier in the week. With that material and Sue's information in hand, Steve, Judy, Lauren, and I met today. We determined that we needed to do the following things before we see Dr. Martin, who has indicated that he's available for a meeting after a summer trip abroad:

- Get an informal commitment from potential volunteers.
- Suggest a sample memo that could be sent to teachers, asking them to identify students in their classes who they felt might benefit from the Books and Breakfast program.
- Talk to community members about volunteering as daily readers. At Orrington, all students in the program are children of color, and Sue felt that readers who are African American or Latino would provide valuable role models.
- Establish where we could set up operations each morning.
- Last, and far from least, explain how we are going to pay for this program.

How *are* we going to pay for this program? From the beginning, Sue, the Groothuises, and Steve and I have been willing to contribute $100 each as seed money. Since we have determined that the program would probably cost $2,000 to $2,500, that $300 seed will have to sprout quickly.

We know we can solicit funds from friends and family members who would support such a program. But we think it is important to show there is support for the program inside the school before we look for outside contributions. Therefore, we'll ask the PTA for a contribution in the fall. If these avenues fail, there is always the publicity route; we figure a well-placed feature article in the local paper or the *Chicago Tribune* or *Sun-Times* would garner us plenty of support.

We have also started listing people we could ask for donations of food, since that would cut our cost. Steve will call on a local bakery supplier we know; Judy volunteered to call the large supermarket down the street from the school, and Lauren offered to call the owner of the newly opened Great Harvest bread store to ask what he does with his overstock.

July 8, 1992

Steve talked on the phone with Dr. Martin, who almost immediately gave us an okay to proceed for the fall. We suggested starting the week after Thanksgiving, since that will give us time to marshal our volunteers, give the teachers time to know their students and determine who would benefit from the program, and give us time to raise the money. Dr. Martin suggested that some money might be available through a school committee, but there was no guarantee.

September 10, 1992

Steve called Dr. Martin, who has attended a principals' meeting and talked to Dr. Wilkins from Orrington and is even more enthusiastic than he was earlier in the summer. He said we would be able to use the gym, which at Kingsley doubles as the lunchroom. We can also have access to refrigerator space in the health clerk's office and the teachers' lounge.

October 26, 1992

We have been busy lining up volunteers. I was a room parent a few times—for both Nora's class and for our oldest daughter, Kate's, class—and although I loved being in the school for holiday parties, I hated all those phone calls trying to get parents to volunteer. Judy, though, is great at phoning and getting things done. Her enthusiasm shamed me into just doing it and swallowing my phobia about calling people.

Surprise! Being a bad phone person pays off. Because I was too shy for cold, cold calls, I phoned people to whom I had mentioned the program or whom I already knew from other school projects. Selective calls assured success. Everyone I asked to commit to serving one day a week said yes. The only hesitation was what to do about the volunteers' younger, preschool children. For now we've decided that the volunteers should ask their own school-age children to remain on the playground during Books and Breakfast, and that bringing along younger siblings is not a good idea. We don't want the servers to be distracted.

A few days ago, Judy asked the supermarket manager if we could get goods free or at reduced prices. He said no, but the sales tax would be waived for our purchases, as we will be affiliated with the school, a not-for-profit institution. This response was a bit disappointing, but we know the chain already participates in a local food bank.

Lauren had better luck with Tom Kolp, the owner of the successful Great Harvest bread store a few blocks from Kingsley. After we supplied him with a one-page letter describing the program, Tom said he'd be glad to call us when he has leftover loaves of his wonderful bread. Unfortunately, he can never be sure in advance when that will be.

Based on these responses, it appears we'll have to pay for most or all of our food. Again money becomes an issue. We will talk to the PTA soon about money, and Dr. Martin is still looking into possible funding sources. How long will we be able to survive on the $300 seed money?

November 10, 1992

Judy, Steve, and I met with Dr. Martin. He had received the go-ahead from the school superintendent, after assuring him that we would not be soliciting the financially strapped school district for funds. We told Dr. Martin that we were ready to go and would like to begin on November 30, then talk to the PTA about the program and ask for funding at their December 1 meeting. Dr. Martin agreed and suggested that we might have another source as well—a local business, CDK Mortgage, which is in the process of "adopting" Kingsley School. He feels confident that CDK will be a source of financial support for us. This good news has taken a heavy burden off our shoulders. We were beginning to think we would have to go hat in hand to friends and relatives.

November 23, 1992

Steve wrote a letter to teacher Audrey Soglin, who is acting as the liaison between Kingsley and CDK Mortgage, inviting her to visit Books and Breakfast.

We have talked among ourselves and to Sue Sussman about the readers and servers in her program. Sue said that she asked an African American police officer she knew to be her very first reader because she felt that his presence would signal to the Orrington boys that it was "cool" to come. She also believed that a male role model, someone who would sit down and read a story at Books and Breakfast, was an important component of the program.

This touched on something we have been concerned about. Almost all the students identified by the Kingsley teachers and staff are African American. How will the kids react to being served by a bunch of largely upper-middle-class white parents? From the beginning we have wanted diversity among volunteers. None of us wants to feel like a little Lady Bountiful coming in with a basket of muffins every day. We want Books and Breakfast to belong to the kids, to make them feel like a healthy and happy part of the school, not to isolate them and make them feel bad about being identified.

Concerned about this, Steve called a successful African American businessman in town. This gentleman, a lifetime resident of Evanston, long involved in politics and the black community, is known not to mince words. Steve explained the Books and Breakfast program and invited the businessman to be one of our first readers. He declined, saying he was too busy at this time to read, but he offered to make a donation. Steve told him we might come back to him later on for that (we've learned since then, never never never turn down money), but right now we were concerned that we might not be doing enough for the kids if we didn't get some role models in immediately.

The businessman put things in perspective. He asked again if these children were hungry. Steve said yes. Okay, he said, then feed them. He explained that when he was growing up in Evanston, a lot of people helped him. Some were black and some were white. It didn't matter to him He said that if the Kingsley kids are truly hungry, we should feed them. If we want to read them a story, that's fine too. But don't worry about the skin color of who's helping.

Here again, no scientific data about what helps a child thrive, just anecdotal evidence. And again, good enough for us. At any rate, members of the African American community do want to get involved. Owen Thomas, the executive director of the Human Relations Commission, has agreed to read the first week, and Tsehaye Hebert of the Arts Council has also signed on.

November 29, 1992

Tom Kolp from Great Harvest called Lauren this morning. He overbaked for Thanksgiving weekend and had sixty-seven loaves of bread. Could we use them?

The program starts tomorrow. Can we use enormous round loaves of delicious, healthy bread made with freshly ground grains, which we can slice, smear peanut butter and jelly on, and cut into square inches of pleasure? Can we use sixty-seven loaves of bread that would save us hundreds of dollars in food costs? Yeah, we might be able to use them.

Judy, Lauren, and I picked up the bread, loaded garbage bags with the individually wrapped loaves, and got on the phone to find freezer space. We could each take five to ten, but that only covered half of the bounty. Diane Bartelt, who has agreed to be a Tuesday morning server, took some and offered her mother's freezer as well. Judy's mother took several, and by day's end we got all the loaves placed.

I think we're set for tomorrow. Judy and I shopped earlier in the week for plates, napkins, and cleaning supplies. The Kingsley PTA has offered us large plastic souvenir cups left over from the school carnival. We will have to wash them every day rather than tossing out paper cups, but washing should go quickly, and this seems slightly more environmentally sound. Most important, it will save us a considerable amount of money.

Diane Bartelt gave us more than freezer space today. She offered to bake muffins every first Tuesday. We had all thought about occasionally baking, but this was a terrific idea. Perhaps people who can't commit to being servers will be willing to bake on a regular basis. That plus the donated bread would cut down dramatically on our food costs.

Speaking of costs, our financial future, while uncertain, is looking up. Judy spoke informally with PTA officers and indicated that we will ask for $500 on December 1. She was told that we will get funding, but it may be closer to $250. Audrey Soglin has also indicated that CDK Mortgage probably will be willing to help. We hope the company will visit and be moved to fund the entire program. Steve insists that once we're up and running and have demonstrated what an important program this is, the school and the community won't let us die for lack of money.

Of course, all this presumes that the children will come—and keep on coming.

November 30, 1992

The first day of Kingsley Books and Breakfast. We sent Kate off to the high school without even asking if she had eaten, and we rushed Nora and our preschooler, Robert, through a spartan breakfast.

We arrived in the gym turned Books and Breakfast room at 8:05. Lauren was right behind us. Judy, as is her style, had already been there for fifteen minutes. Mr. Harris, the school's maintenance engineer, greeted us and said he would provide any help we needed.

Teachers had identified twenty-four children for the program. Dr. Martin sent a letter home with each of these kids last week—a simple explanation of the program and an invitation to participate in the Books and Breakfast club, at no cost. Parents and guardians of these children who wished to help with or visit the club were asked to call us.

Chez Books and Breakfast does not require reservations, so we didn't know how many students would come this first day, or at all. But Dr. Martin and Kingsley secretary Joy Dubner greeted us at the door with the reassuring news that we'd have at least four young participants. The Vaughan brothers (grades five, four, two, and kindergarten), who walked to school, had been peering into Dr. Martin's ground-floor window since before 8 A.M., asking if it was time for breakfast.

The before-school day-care group, which did not overlap with those identified as hungry by the teachers, was just finishing up their morning snack when we arrived. As soon as they left, we set out food, drinks, cups, and napkins and, like nervous host and hostesses, awaited the kids.

The Vaughan brothers arrived first. They filled their plates and sat down, looking a little wary. Terry, the fourth-grader, had a copy of Jack London's *Call of the Wild* with him; he had brought the book he was reading to Books and Breakfast. We were delighted.

At 8:35, all was still quiet. Then the gym door opened and kids started inching in. A bus had arrived. We greeted them all, wanting to learn their names as soon as possible. Some were shy, some were immediately affectionate, and a few were suspicious, as if they were looking for some kind of catch.

By the time the school bell rang, fifteen children had come in and stayed. I read the first chapter of E. B. White's *Stuart Little.* As the kids left, we encouraged them to come back every morning and bring the others who had been invited. Cleanup took about fifteen minutes.

We did it. It is going to work!

December 1, 1992

Steve was not particularly nervous about going to the PTA meeting and asking for Books and Breakfast funding. Having written up a fact sheet that described the who, what, where, when, and why of the program, he felt that getting money would be simple I'm not sure if this is a gender thing or not, but Judy, Lauren, and I were much more apprehensive. We had all attended PTA meetings before—we knew that money was usually tight, and often even small funding decisions were hotly contested and questioned.

Steve and Judy both spoke. After running the program for a whole two days, we felt we already had it under control. Hungry kids—feed them, read to them, and form a lifelong link between learning and nourishment. What's not to like? We were asking for $500 and hoping for at least $250.

After we presented the request, there were questions. How many kids? Twenty-four to infinity. Will you turn kids away? We hope never to do that. How does this affect the whole school? For the school to function at its best, as a community of learners, each student has to have an even chance; Books and Breakfast is one element in leveling the playing field. How much money do you want? Five hundred dollars, but we'll take whatever you decide to give us, and we will continue the program no matter what.

A woman whom I did not recognize raised her hand. She offered an eloquent argument for a program such as Books and Breakfast, saying that although it might not be immediately obvious that her children, who breakfasted at home, would benefit, she knew that each and every child in the school would benefit. She endorsed giving Books and Breakfast the entire $500. I wanted to hug her.

Her motion carried unanimously. Now we have $800, less what we've already spent—enough to carry us into 1993.

Judy also had the wisdom to bring a pad of paper to send around for a volunteer sign-up for bakers and readers. By the end of the meeting we had several reader volunteers and over twenty-five bakers offering to provide muffins once a month. This means that we will have muffins for every day of Books and Breakfast, all year long.

December 2, 1992

On this, our third day, Audrey Soglin brought a guest to Books and Breakfast, a representative from CDK Mortgage. Our original fifteen students had grown to about thirty. Not all of them are on our list, but some of the teachers never submitted names, and some of the kids now coming who weren't identified are siblings of those who were on the list. We have agreed not to turn anyone away as long as they behave, and we have Dr. Martin's support on this. There will be no needs test.

Because our scheduled reader had been called away on business at the last minute, I was reading again. I hadn't noticed our guests come in, and felt that I was losing the attention of the kids and losing my voice trying to be heard in the cavernous gym. I had come to a part in the book where the family is searching for the lost Stuart Little, calling out, "Stuart, Stuart!" I asked all the kids to call out with me. Audience participation was a hit!

After the bell rang, I joined Judy, who was talking to Donna Doberstein, the D in CDK. How much did we want? she asked. We asked for $1,500. And that's how much we got.

December 4, 1992

We are funded and kids are being fed. This should be the end of the story, but a few things are troublesome. Judy and I have noticed that our own kids are acting a bit cranky. Robert still doesn't seem to mind going to his school half an hour earlier than before, but it is tough getting him going in the morning. Nora does not want to hang out on the playground before school. It's December, with no snow yet. The playground is cold and boring. It isn't fair to make her and Elizabeth stay outside, she says. She's right.

Even Kate, from her long-distance teenage vantage point, made a joking remark when she saw me baking muffins last night. "Are those for Books and Breakfast or for us? We're your real children, Mom." She was kidding, but it still struck a chord. Judy and I have been talking about nothing else but Books and Breakfast. We need to loosen up with Nora and Elizabeth—let them hang out in the gym, to read their own books, listen to the story, help, whatever.

We aren't doing our families any good by rushing everybody out the door—our own children are barely having breakfast. Luckily, Judy and I are close enough friends that we can talk each other through tense times. Also, we keep reminding each other that we don't have to go every day. Not that we listen to each other. Judy works a rotating schedule at the hospital—one week she might work three days, then no days for the next two weeks. I teach at the University of Illinois, but my first class isn't until 11 A.M., so I'm flexible most mornings. Steve writes in an office about ten minutes away from the school. He has always liked to arrive there very early, but he insists that he doesn't mind getting there after 9 A.M. now because of Books and Breakfast.

We're all hooked. We organized the volunteer servers and readers so that we wouldn't have to come every day. And we don't have to, because the daily servers are great. But we've already fallen in love with the kids. And we have come to realize that the consistency of having a few of us there every day or almost every day is almost as important as the peanut butter and jelly and orange segments.

We have begun to get daily hugs from some of the kids, warmer than some of us get from our own kids on some mornings, and we are reaping the rewards that all volunteers working with children must come to know: satisfaction in doing something worthwhile and unconditional love for something as small and as matter-of-fact as handing someone a glass of juice and telling him to have a good day at school.

December 7, 1992

Steve had the idea of adding hard-boiled eggs to our morning menu. He has already claimed it as his specialty and made two dozen for today. I thought the kids would turn up their noses, but he was right—they loved the eggs, and we ran out immediately. Steve promises more one or two days next week.

Daily hugs are great and they continue, but there are some kids with serious troubles here, too. One boy in particular looks far older than his seven years and seems much too tough for a second-grader. Every day he eats something—today he gobbled up two of the eggs—but when I suggested he move over to the table and listen to the story, he just shook his head. He is suspicious or angry or cold or something I can't imagine.

I talked to Steve about him every day last week—he stands out in his hostility. I'm usually a Pollyanna about this kind of thing, but this guy seems lost already. In second grade he seems hardened to anyone around him who might want to be kind. His face and his future are haunting.

A lawyer friend arranged for Steve to talk with his client Bill Rickman, the head of the Kroch's and Brentano's bookstore chain. We wondered if the Evanston store would donate books we could give to the kids at Christmas—a present for staying in the club. Mr. Rickman had a better idea. The kids could visit the store to see how it worked—and to pick out inexpensive books. We're set for Saturday, December 19. Now we must start thinking about the logistics, the permission slips, the chaperons, the transportation.

December 8, 1992

We received an unsolicited $100 check from a Kingsley family. Steve will deposit it at the First Illinois bank where we set up a checking account. He is handling the checkbook and legal paperwork. He previously made sure we were incorporated in the state of Illinois as a not-for-profit corporation. The documents seemed rather simple. We had to set up a board of directors—Judy, Lauren, Steve, and me—elect officers, provide a statement about what we do, sign on the dotted line a few times, and send the secretary of state $50.

Upon learning that we are a not-for-profit in the area that it serves, the bank waived all checking fees and said we do not have to maintain a minimum balance. The young banker, who had no idea that kids at the school four blocks away were hungry, provided temporary checks and said that if we didn't want to spend our money on inscribed checks, he'd keep on providing temporary ones. A nice gesture.

December 10, 1992

After all my inner turmoil about losing our children so early, our troubled second-grader seems to be coming around. He doesn't seem to be so unreachable now—he asks Steve every day when he's bringing more hard-boiled eggs.

December 14, 1992

Our hard-boiled second-grader returned his permission slip and can't stop asking us about the field trip. He's made Steve his special friend, and I return as Pollyanna. He gives us all a huge hug every day.

December 19, 1992

Field trip! Twenty-one permission slips were returned to us, but only nine kids showed up. We had six chaperons and drivers, so it was pretty close to a one-on-one experience. It would have been a perfect "photo op"—nine kids being treated to a holiday tour of the bookstore, leaving with their own books, etc., but we decided not to try for any publicity here. What purpose would it serve other than to massage our egos? The program is fully funded, and we could not be certain how a newspaper or television station would characterize the kids. At risk? Disadvantaged? Behavioral problems? None of these would be wholly accurate. To us they're just kids, and we can't justify subjecting them to embarrassment or exploitation by reporters looking for an angle.

April 19, 1993

The program has become so much a part of our lives that it hardly seems necessary to keep a diary anymore. But there is much worth mentioning—those hugs, our increasing speed at cranking out peanut butter sandwiches, volunteer server Jeanie Ramsey's homemade cinnamon rolls as a B and B treat, the cooperation of the staff and teachers at Kingsley, readers Judith Treadway and Gwen Poole and their introduction of ethnic folktales, the focus that Books and Breakfast has given to the lives of all those involved.

But questions have come up. Some parents of children not in the program have questioned the policy of never turning anyone away. It's true we don't administer a needs test. Some of our kids might have breakfast available to them, but there's some reason that they like to come every morning. We want them to feel like they belong.

Also, how do you say, *No, you're not poor enough!* How are we isolating the kids whom we do serve? Would we be stigmatizing them unfairly?

We were also asked if we were enabling families not to serve their own children breakfast. Our answer: How does that question apply? We have no political agenda. Our purpose is not to judge the families of these children; our goal is to feed hungry children. We think we are achieving the goal. A school staff person spotted one of our kids and said she didn't think that he was hungry, that he was just coming to Books and Breakfast to avoid conflicts on the playground. Hurray! We gladly expand the definition of *feeding a need* to include that!

May 11, 1993

Permission slips are due—we're taking the kids on another field trip, this time to the Art Institute of Chicago on a school day. Judy's mother leads school tours there, and we received a special contribution from Mike McCluggage, an attorney at Steve's old firm, to cover the cost of the bus and the sack lunches. We are cautiously optimistic about our ability to pull this off; there will be a lot more kids and a lot fewer chaperones than on our trip to the bookstore.

May 18, 1993

Our field trip was a disaster. We had expected to take forty-one kids with eight chaperons. But this morning ten more students brought permission slips and two chaperons did not show up. Our hope of having one teacher along also didn't materialize. We were outnumbered, outenergized, and outwitted. This was our big mistake of the year.

We have learned one of those major life lessons—do what you do well. We do excellent Books and Breakfast. We do not do field trips well.

June 9, 1993

Our last day. With the warm weather and the excitement of the end of the school year, our numbers have decreased. On some winter days we fed as many as fifty-five kids; lately it has been half that. Funny, feeding only twenty-five or thirty kids now seems so easy, but on our first day, six months ago, we thought fifteen was a lot.

We've asked all the children to come, promising them a surprise. Maybe the biggest surprise was ours this week. Our hard-boiled second-grader came in and slipped an orange into Steve's pocket. "Here's breakfast for you today," he said, smiling.

Forty kids came for our last breakfast. We handed out books secured through Sue Sussman and our own publisher and promised to see everyone next year. And we got those incredible hugs, which would have to last us through the summer.

Postscript

When school ended, we determined that we had served over 6,500 meals to 81 different students over the year for a little more than $1,500—about twenty-five cents per meal. I wish we could give our own children muffins, Great Harvest bread and peanut butter, fruit, and milk for that price.

Books and Breakfast will be a Kingsley PTA committee for the 1993–94 school year. Judy, Steve, and I will chair the program. Most of our servers, bakers, and readers will be back. And I'm quite sure that we will organize the program to run so smoothly that we won't have to be there every day.

We will then proceed to be there every day.

Resource Guide

There are a wealth of organizations that facilitate volunteerism in virtually every community across America. The United Way, churches and synagogues, local PTAs, and service organizations such as the Kiwanis and Junior League, among others, are excellent starting places for the individual or family looking to make a difference. In addition to these and other institutions, there are volunteer centers and government-related initiatives that make getting involved relatively easy. Readers may want to contact the following organizations.

POINTS OF LIGHT FOUNDATION

The foundation is an independent, not-for-profit organization dedicated to mobilizing leaders from all sectors of society to motivate their members for community service. Not a grant-making organization, the foundation works through the media, businesses, government, not-for-profit organizations, and four hundred volunteer centers and sixty-six corporate volunteer councils across the country to serve as a catalyst for community service initiatives.

To learn more about the foundation or find the center or council closest to your community, contact
Points of Light Foundation, 736 Jackson Place NW,
Washington, D.C. 20503.
Phone: 202-408-5162.

CITY CARES OF AMERICA

This rapidly growing not-for-profit organization has created a community service model that engages busy, working people in direct-service, team volunteer projects with a variety of schedules and time commitments. Hands on Atlanta, profiled earlier in this book, is an example of the City Cares organizations that currently exist in cities including Austin, Baltimore, Boston, Charlotte, Chicago, Dallas, Detroit, Los Angeles, Memphis, Nashville, New York, Phoenix, Pittsburgh, San Diego, and Washington, D.C. At this writing, groups are also being formed in Miami, New Jersey, New Orleans, Philadelphia, and Seattle

For more information on volunteering with a local City Cares group or on starting one in your area, contact
City Cares of America, P.O. Box 27595, Washington, D.C. 20038.
Phone: 202-887-0500.

CORPORATION FOR NATIONAL AND COMMUNITY SERVICE

The corporation, the centerpiece of President Bill Clinton's national service program, has the mandate to engage Americans of all ages and backgrounds in community-based service. In doing so, the corporation will foster civic responsibility and provide educational opportunity for those who make a substantial commitment to service. A new national initiative, the AmeriCorps program, builds upon the strong network of existing national service programs of not-for-profit organizations by supporting locally driven projects. Part-time and full-time AmeriCorps participants receive a limited wage while serving and a post-service award to be used for past or present education expenses.

The corporation functions as a clearinghouse of information and technical expertise for service initiatives nationwide and as a service "venture capitalist," providing funding on a competitive basis for state and national service programs. The corporation also enhances service-learning programs in K–12 schools and higher-education institutions, as well as programs that utilize the talents of older Americans.

For further information, contact
The Corporation for National and Community Service,
1100 Vermont Ave. NW, Washington, D.C. 20525.

Acknowledgments

The authors were helped in more than fifty ways by more than fifty people. Our thanks and admiration go first to those who are profiled on these pages. They give selflessly of their time to better their communities, and they gave selflessly of their time to better this book.

Many others deserve recognition. Eli Segal and his able assistant Jodi Kanter were of great service. So, too, were Kathy Quilty and Miah Homstad of the Points of Light Foundation. Morris Dees, Tom Fiffer, and George Rosic also provided special assistance.

Our literary agent Gordon Kato believed in the project from day one and was essential in not only finding the right publisher, but in shaping the content. Our editor Rob Robertson was a writer's dream. Always accessible, he provided editorial focus and moral support, and worked tirelessly and creatively to ensure that the book's message be spread far and wide.

It would have been impossible to complete this book without the assistance and patience of friends and family. Special thanks to Kate, Nora, and Robert Fiffer and to Judy Groothuis. And special, special thanks to our parents for teaching us the importance of community service. It is a legacy that we shall continue.

About the Authors

Steve and Sharon Sloan Fiffer, both forty-three, are the parents of three children. Steve is the author of numerous books including *A Season for Justice* and *Hate on Trial,* both with Morris Dees, and *So You've Got a Great Idea* and *How to Watch Baseball.* Sharon is the co–executive editor of the literary magazine *Other Voices,* and the author of *Imagining America,* which was honored by the New York Public Library as one of the 100 Outstanding Books for Young Adults.

Made in the USA
Lexington, KY
12 March 2015